In Search of Home

ISBN: 978-1-885270-74-0

Cover Design: Kristi Yoder

First Printing: March 2008

Printed in the USA

For more information about Christian Aid Ministries, see page 235.

To order additional copies of *In Search of Home* please contact:

TGS International
PO Box 355
Berlin, Ohio 44610 USA
Phone: 330·893·4828
Fax: 330·893·2305
Email: tgsbooks@camoh.org

TGS#000017
HG#12823

In Search of Home

by Harvey Yoder

Table of Contents

Foreword...7

Chapter 1 9

Chapter 2 19

Chapter 3 35

Chapter 4 41

Chapter 5 49

Chapter 6 57

Chapter 7 67

Chapter 8 77

Chapter 9 87

Chapter 10...97

Chapter 11...105

Chapter 12...115

Chapter 13...125

Chapter 14...135

Chapter 15...143

Chapter 16...153

Chapter 17...165

Chapter 18...175

Chapter 19...185

Chapter 20...193

Chapter 21...205

Chapter 22...211

Chapter 23...221

Epilogue 227

Glossary 231

Foreword

How thankful we are to our gracious heavenly Father for guiding us into His fold! He has so kindly shown His love to us in so many ways. We are thankful for the difficulties and tests He has brought into our lives. "And we know that all things work together for good to them that love God, to them who are the called according to his purpose" (Rom. 8:28). We allowed our story to be told, not to bring honor and glory to ourselves, but to magnify the name of our Lord Jesus.

Abdullah and Zumrat Jousoupjanov

Chapter 1

As the dismissal bell clanged throughout the large public school building, pupils poured from the classrooms into the central hall. They rushed for their next classes, barely even hearing the hum of city traffic outside. Their chattering voices and leather-shod feet turned their environment into a world of its own—the world of school.

As the students passed each other in the corridors, one dark-haired, seventh-grade boy stepped out of a group of boys and headed for the flow of students coming the other way. His alert eyes had seen a cluster of girls approaching, and had singled out one girl in particular.

Zumrat* was not looking at anyone. She saw the bobbing heads only as part of the daily scene. As usual, she was on the edge of the cluster of girls, not joining in the chatter with her classmates. But her space was invaded when Monat walked up to her and in a brazen voice joked, "I would really like you if you were as pretty as you look! Outside, you are beautiful enough to eat, but inside, you are cold!"

The boys hooted with laughter at their leader's jibe

* Please see glossary on pages 231–232 for pronunciations of words.

and gathered around the two in a semi-circle. Monat turned his head to accept the adulation of his peers—a mistake he would immediately regret.

At first Zumrat had just glared at the offender, but then, with a determined step forward, she grabbed Monat's shirtfront and pushed him across the hall and against the wall. The boy hardly knew what had hit him. He looked into Zumrat's steeled black eyes only inches from his own as she hissed, "You stop pestering me, do you hear? No more pulling my hair! No more smart remarks about me!" Her voice was low and ominous.

The buzz of voices behind them reminded Monat of the other students in the hall. His own temper flared and he kicked out at Zumrat, trying to upset her balance.

With a swift movement the girl grabbed his leg, and Monat fell onto the tile floor in an undignified heap. Then he grunted as the enraged girl sat right on his stomach and began pummeling his head and shoulders.

"If you don't leave me alone, I will do even worse things to you!" she panted between swings.

Then a strong arm reached out and a teacher's hand grabbed Zumrat. "Enough! Young lady, march yourself straight to the principal's office!"

Zumrat's face was flushed as she stood up and released her victim. Monat picked himself up from the floor.

***

The principal's room was large and airy. The tall windows were closed against the bitter winter weather that swept down from the mountains in Kyrgyzstan and over the city of Osh. Three people were in the office.

"Mrs. Ivanov, your daughter has been reprimanded numerous times for her behavior. We have called you in to warn you that if she does not stop her uncalled-for behavior, we will have to take disciplinary measures." The principal was a woman, yet it was clear that she was well suited to her position. She held her head erect over her squared shoulders and her steady eyes stared straight at Zumrat's mother.

"I apologize for Zumrat's behavior," Sopia replied, clearly disturbed by her daughter's actions. "I will give immediate attention to this unfortunate matter."

Zumrat sat on a wooden chair beside her mother, her long, dark lashes hiding her eyes as she studied her hands, which were clasped together on the dark blue skirt of her school uniform. Her face showed no emotion whatsoever.

"Zumrat!" The principal's voice cut straight across the desk toward the girl. "I want to hear no more of your rough and rowdy ways! Do you hear?"

"Yes, ma'am." The girl's voice was not too loud, not too soft. *Rather defiant*, the principal thought as she looked hard at her student.

"You will apologize," her mother hissed at her, clearly upset by her daughter's lack of respect for the principal.

"I am sorry I caused a disturbance," Zumrat said quickly. She had expected this and was prepared to make a statement. That was what they always wanted—a statement. And she had learned the diplomatic way of saying she was sorry without actually being sorry for what she had done.

"A disturbance! It was more than a disturbance! It was a fight!" Once more the principal's voice cut through the air.

"I will take care of it!" Sopia was almost begging. "I will make sure that Zumrat behaves herself." Her eyes flashed from her daughter's stoic countenance back to the principal's cold eyes.

Suddenly the principal stood. "See that you do," she said, dismissing them with a wave of her hand.

All the way home from school, Zumrat felt her mother's displeasure. When they reached their house, her mother's fury erupted. As the words washed over her, Zumrat said very little. She just stood in the doorway of the kitchen and watched her mother scurry around making the evening meal.

No one had asked her why she had hit Monat. No one was interested in that side of the story. It did not seem to matter that Monat had been harassing her relentlessly ever since the school term had begun. The day before he had tweaked her hair. She had decided then and there to stand up for herself, since she knew no one else would help her. Hadn't she seen what happened when bullies in school made life miserable for their victims? Well, she was not going to become one of those timid girls who avoided the hallways and were always on the lookout for their tormentors. It had only taken a few months for Zumrat to see that the teachers did not seem to care what went on among the students. They kept strict rule in the classrooms, but the halls and the playground were open to cruelty and bullying. Zumrat had known what she must do the first time she was given the opportunity, and today had been the day.

She had been in a number of scrapes at the beginning of the year, but those clashes had been with the leaders among the girls, and she had quickly taught them to leave her alone.

The Soviet system that had taken over the country of Kyrgyzstan and gradually established its value systems for over fifty years did not concern Zumrat. She only knew that in her thirteenth year, in 1974, she had to come up with her own value system—one that allowed her to survive.

Today she had learned something else. She would have to make sure that any future disputes took place in a more private location. She was sure she would have to defend herself again. Victory usually did not come that easily.

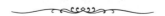

Adjusting the burner of the kerosene stove, Zumrat tested

the water inside the pail. She looked out the window where her father was cleaning the car. Her mother was still not home from her teaching job at the elementary school, and Zumrat had been at home alone until her father had driven in. Her sisters were at their grandmother's house on the next street. But Zumrat did not mind being alone. A loner by nature, she spent long hours by herself, reading or just wandering around the city sidewalks. She did not need much time to do her homework, for studies came easily for her.

When the water was warm, Zumrat carried the pail carefully out the side door and set it down beside the car. Mild spring weather made it a special treat to be outside after the cold winter.

"Thank you." Zumrat's father smiled at his daughter. "You always know just what I need even before I ask."

Zumrat smiled back. Like him, she was quiet and paid attention to details. She felt a special bond between them.

Her father began washing the car with a sponge. He was a taxi driver, and a clean car often brought him additional customers. The state system pay was adequate, but sometimes generous customers tipped, and the additional funds were quite welcome.

Bending over, Zumrat picked up an empty pail and went to bring clean water to rinse the car. Father and daughter worked side by side in companionable silence.

But Zumrat's mind was busy. How was it that her mother did not seem to understand her moods, when her father was so sympathetic with how she felt about life? Her mother had been so upset about her fight with Monat. When her father had come home while her mother was still in her tirade, he had told her to stop. Later he had wanted to know what Monat had done to upset her. He had said very little, and even though she sensed he was not happy about the fight, it meant much that he had at least listened to her.

Dashing clean water over the hood of the car, Zumrat thought of how the school bullies had left her alone after that fight. To her surprise, she had even become somewhat of a champion among the downtrodden. Only two weeks after the incident, she had been leaving the schoolhouse when she saw a cluster of girls between two buildings.

"Leave her alone," she had said in a determined voice when she saw that the girls were tormenting a classmate.

The knot of girls had turned, surprised by the authority in her voice. When they had hesitated, Zumrat had balled up her fists, and after the girls had scattered, she had told the trembling victim, "You have to stand up for yourself. No one else will help you."

The girl had been too scared to say anything, but somehow word spread and the students learned to fear the aloof, stony-faced girl. In the later years of high school, Zumrat actually became friends with a number of girls who admired her fearlessness and ability to fight for her rights.

"Why can't you come with us to the party?" The girls crowded around Zumrat, begging her with eager voices.

The graduation party that evening was to be a big event. Even Zumrat, who usually avoided big gatherings and crowds, wanted to attend.

"I have to work. My father is adding another room onto our house and my mom wants me to move all the bricks to that side of the house. It will take all evening," Zumrat informed them without much feeling. Sure, she wanted to go to the party, but life had taught her not to set her heart too much on anything. There were too many disappointments.

"We'll help you," Margreta told her. She looked at the other girls for confirmation. An eager chorus agreed.

For a moment Zumrat said nothing. Then she asked slowly, "You will come and help move the bricks? There are hundreds!"

In reply, her friends gathered around her and began walking toward Zumrat's home.

Heedless of the cars going by, Zumrat's mother walked from the bus stop toward home. Her day had been busy as usual, keeping order among the elementary students in her classroom and trying to force information into heads that sometimes seemed stuffed with Styrofoam, all the while maintaining a professional attitude.

She was almost home when she saw an amazing scene right in her own yard. Two long lines of girls, more than twenty in all, were rapidly handing bricks from one to the next. The line stretched from the front of the house all the way around the side, where Sopia saw Zumrat taking the bricks from the last girl and stacking them onto a growing pile.

Grabbing hold of the fence in her surprise, Sopia called out, "What is going on?"

"Oh, ma'am, we are helping Zumrat so she can go with us to the graduation party!" one laughing girl replied, handing another brick to the next girl in line. "We couldn't bear the thought of our friend having to miss this important event!"

Sopia gathered herself and walked into the yard. She saw Zumrat's flushed face as she rapidly stacked the bricks. "What is going on?" Sopia asked. "How in the world did you make these girls come and work for you?"

"I didn't, Mama," Zumrat said, straightening briefly and looking directly into her mother's face. "They insisted."

"That I find hard to believe," Sopia replied, shaking her head. She looked in bewilderment at the hard-working girls, busily passing the bricks from one to the other. At the rate they were moving, the work would soon be done. The yard was filled with girlish chatter and laughter.

"This is ridiculous," Sopia managed to say. She looked sharply at Zumrat, suddenly seeing her daughter in a new light. No longer just a schoolgirl, Zumrat was rapidly becoming a young lady—an attractive young lady.

"I will go, Mama," Zumrat said calmly, looking at her mother. "You wanted the bricks moved, and they are moved. You know Daddy would let me go."

Sopia was speechless. *How dare she?* But as she met her daughter's steady gaze, she had to come to grips with the fact that her daughter was almost grown up. If someone had asked Sopia why she did not want her daughter to go to the graduation party, she would not have known what to say. Was she trying to stop time as she watched her children grow up? Did she, like so many parents, want to maintain control over her mature children as she had when they were young?

Zumrat sensed her mother's inner struggle, so she said one more time, "I am going to my graduation party. The girls came to help me with my work so I could go, and I will not disappoint them."

"I still don't know how you convinced so many girls to come and help with such dirty work!" Sopia sputtered, trying to make sense of the confusion. "I didn't know you had so many friends. It's incredible!"

Zumrat said nothing, but a slow smile spread across her face. She herself wasn't sure how it had happened. Since she was not a social butterfly, talking and chattering with ease in school, she, too, was surprised to find that she was respected and well liked.

Zumrat did not especially enjoy the graduation party, but she ate the prepared food and danced with her classmates. At midnight she excused herself and went home. She had made up her mind beforehand that she was not going to stay late and become involved with the late night crowd.

Was it worth it? She asked herself on the way home. She nodded slightly. Yes, it had been worth it. Now that part of her life was over and she would move on—on into the future, whatever that might be.

Chapter 2

The shadows lengthened as the evening sun extended warm fingers through the window and across the bed. The radio played lively folk tunes, and the two girls sitting on the bed looking at a fashion magazine swayed slightly to the lilting melodies.

Zumrat looked appreciatively around her friend Rano's room. She liked it here. Her own home was nice enough, but Rano's parents must have done well in their careers. She did not know where Rano's father worked, but he was always dressed in a business suit and seemed very important.

"What are you thinking?" Rano laughed, looking at Zumrat's serious face. "Are you wondering what boy is going to ask you next? You have had quite a string of wannabes!" She laughed and tossed her dark hair.

Zumrat grinned and gave her friend a sideways shove. "No! I was just thinking of how nice your room is. Your entire house," she added.

"Thanks! Yeah, we have a nice house, but it sure does get lonely sometimes." Rano was an only child.

"I have an idea!" Rano bounced on the bed. "You should become a part of the family! Then I would see you more often!" With a bound, she jumped off the bed and took several steps toward her dresser. Rummaging around in her top drawer, she triumphantly brought out a black and white photo of a young man. "This is my cousin, Abdullah, and you should marry him! Then you would almost be my sister!" Rano giggled and shoved the picture in front of Zumrat.

Taking a quick glance at the photo, Zumrat shrugged. "Not interested," she said without a second glance. "I don't like the way he looks."

"Oh, you!" Rano tried to sound angry. "You never like anyone! The boys want to take you out, and you always turn them down. Look, Abdullah is a good-looking man! He is older than you are, but you always seemed more mature than the rest of us. You should consider him. I want to tell him about you."

Zumrat tried to smile. As much as she liked her friend, she was not going to let Rano choose her husband. She looked once more at the picture. Black hair and a brown complexion, a black drooping mustache and a sober look—he was obviously from Kyrgyzstan like herself. That was all she could see from the photo.

Handing it back to Rano, Zumrat repeated, "Not interested. He looks rather homely to me."

Grabbing her friend's shoulders, Rano lamented, "What will we do with you? You are the most eligible girl in our group, and you refuse to look at any of the young men. What is wrong with you?" Even though she asked playfully, Zumrat heard the hint of impatience in her friend's voice.

"I don't know," Zumrat said in her calm, slow voice. "I don't know what's wrong with me."

The music continued playing. The two girls fell silent once more.

Unbidden, Zumrat's thoughts flew back to the week before. By herself in her own room, a great feeling of loneliness had swept over her. She had not known what was going on inside of her.

She had turned on the radio, and, as the Soviet orchestra played some classical piece, she had begun to weep. She could not have explained to anyone—even to herself—why she was crying. She just felt a great emptiness in her heart.

"So, when will you marry?" Rano was insistent.

With a dry chuckle, Zumrat said, "I will tell you what I told my mother when she asked me that question."

"What's that?" Rano asked.

"I told her I am going to marry a man in the military and have ten children. I will not live in Osh all my life."

With a delighted laugh, Rano asked, "Whatever made you say that?" She rocked on the bed with glee.

"I don't know, really," Zumrat laughed in reply. "I just got tired of her asking me."

"You are quite the case," Rano said. "A military man and ten children! No one has that many children anymore. At least not modern people."

"Yeah, my mom thinks it's a dreadful shame to have an old maid in the house. She made a comment just the other day— 'Already twenty-two years old and still no man.' Well, I tell you, I am in no hurry."

"You really should consider Abdullah," Rano insisted as she rescued the rejected photo from the floor where it had fallen. She studied her cousin's face and shrugged her shoulders. Her chin lifted slightly. "He really is much better looking in real life." There was a gleam in her eye as she stashed the photo in her drawer.

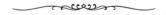

With a quick stride, Zumrat climbed the steps to the store where she worked as a clerk. She was just returning from her lunch break in the park. As the door closed behind her, blocking out the noise from the city, one of her coworkers looked up from behind the counter.

"So now you come!" Tanya said with a grin. "After the tall, dark, handsome man has left!"

Zumrat didn't respond as she calmly walked around the counter and joined her partner.

"You keep all the boys away so you can go out with this man?" Tanya giggled. "You are quite the case!"

"What do you mean?" Zumrat asked, used to the teasing remarks of the other girls who worked with her.

"Oh, ho," Tanya giggled. "Now you pretend you don't know. You can't fool me! When this nice man came in and looked around, I asked him what he needed. 'Is Zumrat here?' he asked so politely."

Zumrat shook her head, but said nothing. She began refolding a stack of towels someone had been looking at. Finally she said, "I don't know anyone like that."

"Well," Tanya laughed again, "he knew about you!"

"Put your mind at ease. I have no man in my life. I don't even know who you're talking about," Zumrat assured her.

"Oh, I'm sure he'll be back," Tanya teased. "He really did seem to want to see you."

Late that same afternoon Tanya hissed, "There he is!" Zumrat continued stocking shelves. With a quick glance, she took in the tall young man looking at some merchandise in the glass case. She ignored him. He loitered about, looking at different items. He looked in her direction more than once, but she studiously avoided letting him catch her eye.

"Excuse me, please." The man's voice was low, yet pleasant. "Could you assist me with my purchase?"

Zumrat turned toward his friendly face. "What is it you need?" She kept her voice even.

"I want to purchase two pairs of socks, please."

Silently Zumrat reached into the showcase and brought out the items he indicated. Even though she felt his gaze on her face, she did not look directly at him. Tanya smirked behind the counter and stared openly at the unfolding drama.

"Keep the change," the young man said with a smile as he handed her the coins to pay for his purchase. "Keep it for yourself."

Zumrat stared straight at him. "You are a strange man," she said shortly.

As he turned to leave, Zumrat looked at the coins in her hand. She stared at his retreating back. When he turned to look at her again, she said, "I don't need your charity," and tossed the coins onto the floor after him. *That should nip any romantic ambitions,* she thought, smirking slightly.

Turning, the young man bent over and picked up the coins. Then, with a small smile in her direction, he left the store.

For the rest of the afternoon Zumrat tried to be stoical in spite of Tanya's teasing. She wanted to brush the entire episode aside.

"Happy birthday, Rano!" Zumrat pushed her friend's door open and walked into her house.

"Oh, thank you!" Rano ran to the door to welcome her friend.

"Here are some flowers for you, and look, I brought you some candy and champagne!" Zumrat gave her friend the gifts and the two girls hugged affectionately.

"Come on in," Rano invited, drawing her toward the living room. "My parents are here and some of my relatives."

Zumrat greeted Rano's parents and took a seat on the sofa beside her friend. Then she studied the rest of the guests. She jumped as her eyes fell on a familiar face. Where had she seen him? Then it came to her. The man in the store! The guy she had called a strange man! He was here—in Rano's house!

"Hi," the young man said with a smile when he saw her looking at him.

She was too embarrassed to respond. Without a word, she got up and escaped into the kitchen.

Rano followed her. "What is it?" she asked with a mischievous grin.

"Who is that?" Zumrat hissed, glaring at her friend.

"That," Rano told her, cocking her head to one side, "is my cousin Abdullah. Remember, I showed you his picture?"

Zumrat felt as though something were choking her. "How could you? I had no idea! He was in the store, and I was rude to him! He must think I'm a terrible girl!" The words sprang from her mouth in uncharacteristic gibberish. Her face burned as she remembered her words to him.

"No, I don't think so," Rano giggled. "He talked about seeing you, and he did not seem at all upset. I think he likes you."

Zumrat took a deep breath. "Likes me?" she echoed in a whisper. "Are you crazy?" She turned and looked out the window.

The chatter of voices from the other room rose as more guests arrived. Zumrat turned to face her friend. "I'm leaving. I—I cannot stay here." And before her astonished friend could argue, Zumrat was out the side door, almost running down the walkway.

"Stupid, stupid, stupid!" Zumrat muttered as her quick steps took her farther and farther from Rano's house. "He must think I am the most heartless, rude person in the world! How could she?" Back and forth her mind darted, first angry with herself for having been rude, and then angry with Rano for having sent that man—what was his name? Abdullah?—to spy on her without her even knowing he was her cousin. Waves of shame swept over her.

She was confused. Why did this upset her so much? She had

given others the cold shoulder. More than once she had clearly let some insistent young man know she was definitely not interested in his attentions. Why was this different?

<hr />

"When will you be free?"

Zumrat looked into the dark eyes regarding her from across the counter and recognized the young man who had been at the party the night before. Abdullah had walked in the door soon after the store had opened.

"At closing time," Zumrat answered quickly. Then she turned away and walked into the back room. When she finally returned to her position by the counter, he had gone. Another wave of shame swept over her.

True, she was free when the store closed, but this was actually her half day. At noon she left the store and walked quickly home. Surely he would get the hint and leave her alone when he returned in the evening and found she was not there.

But no, the next day he was back again in the afternoon, just before closing time, wandering around the store. When Zumrat hissed at Tanya in a low voice and asked what she had told him, Tanya lifted her shoulders in pretended innocence and smirked.

"I waited for you yesterday," Abdullah said quietly when she walked out of the store at closing time.

"I left at noon," Zumrat replied shortly.

"I know."

The two walked down the sidewalk in silence. Abdullah made small talk about the weather and life in the city. Zumrat replied occasionally, but before they reached the street where she lived, she pointedly told him, "You don't need to come with me any farther." She definitely did not want anyone from her family to see him.

Abdullah took the hint and watched her walk away.

But the next evening he was waiting for her and again walked her to the same spot. Then he disappeared for a week.

Zumrat tried to tell herself she was not at all concerned. She did not look for him after work for the first couple of days. But by the third day, she glanced up and down the street. She could see nothing of Abdullah. He had vanished.

Ahh, she was glad! Yes, she really was. Finally that embarrassing episode was behind her. She was relieved—really she was.

———————

"Oh, Abdullah! Yes, I know him," Nadia said quickly. Zumrat had met her old classmate on the sidewalk, and for some reason Zumrat had asked her if she knew a young man named Abdullah. "He works in the same school where I work. He is very smart," Nadia said admiringly.

The next time Zumrat saw her classmate, Nadia's tone was different. "What are you doing, taking away my boyfriend? I told him you had asked me about him, and he started talking about how pretty and smart you are!" Her eyes sparked as she spoke.

"You can have him! I am not trying to take anyone's boyfriend!" Zumrat said scornfully, then turned away. She was not one of those girls who were constantly on the lookout for men, especially not other girls' boyfriends!

So the next week, when she saw Abdullah waiting once more outside the store, Zumrat was cool and distant. She hardly spoke and tried to make it plain that she was not interested. That evening, when Rano came over to "see how it was going," she disappointed her friend by saying nothing was going.

But the next evening, her faithful suitor once more presented himself and proceeded to walk her home.

"Why don't you leave me alone?" Zumrat asked bluntly after they had walked several blocks. It was plain that he really was trying to woo her. "Why don't you go back to your girlfriend and leave me alone?"

There was no immediate response, only the sound of their footsteps on the concrete sidewalk.

"I don't have a girlfriend," came the steady reply. "Why do you think I have anyone else?"

Oh, great! she thought. *Anyone else. Not only does he deny it, he now considers himself my boyfriend!*

"Nadia told me to leave you alone. She said I was trying to steal her boyfriend."

More silence.

"Nadia is a silly girl. Just because she wants to be my girlfriend does not mean I want her. She is silly, like many girls are."

Zumrat said nothing as she tried to sort out her feelings. At least it helped to know he was not two-timing her. But the rest of the walk was still uncomfortable, and Zumrat was relieved when they reached her corner.

The walks continued. Every day after work her faithful escort was waiting. Zumrat knew he was becoming more and more serious, yet she did not really think she wanted to continue. She was bewildered and had difficulty knowing how to respond to his attentions.

Abdullah told her about his boyhood and his life. Raised in a family of mostly boys, he was the typical product of Osh. His father was an actor in the theater and specialized in drama. His mother was a worker in some other part of the city. Nothing of particular interest made his life outstanding. He did have a good job teaching, so his future seemed secure.

But Zumrat was definitely not prepared to answer Abdullah's proposal with a "yes" when only a week later he said, "I want you to be my girl. I want to marry you!"

She answered with a definite, "No."

"Don't tell me 'no,'" Abdullah teased her, yet she could hear how serious he was. "If you tell me 'no,' I will tell your parents that if you are suddenly gone, it is because I have eloped with you!"

With a grunt, Zumrat said, "Do you think that will make me say 'yes'? I say 'no' again. Not now, or ever."

This silenced him for a while. But for some reason, when they arrived at the corner where they usually parted, Abdullah turned and followed Zumrat home. Quite aware of his footsteps following her, Zumrat tried to walk briskly, thinking perhaps she could shake off the persistent young man who was so intent on winning her heart.

"Why do you follow me?" she asked when he drew up beside her.

"Zumrat, I love you! Don't you understand?"

She did not look at his face. "I already said 'no'! You don't understand that word?"

With a chuckle, Abdullah replied, "I am trying to read your heart, not the words you speak. I think there is a difference."

"I don't know my own heart," Zumrat said with a wry laugh. "How can you know it?"

"Because I think I understand some things about a certain young lady that she herself doesn't understand. With half a chance, I could teach her much about herself." Even though his voice was light, Zumrat knew he was serious.

"The neighbors will see you!" Zumrat was getting agitated. "They will all think that I am . . . that I am . . . your girlfriend!"

"Then I think I like your neighbors," Abdullah laughed.

"My family! My mom won't let me rest if she sees you walk me home! She is always talking to me about . . . about . . ." her voice trailed off into nothing.

"I want to see your mother. And your father. In fact, I want to meet all of your family and your relatives. I want you to meet my family. I want to marry you!"

Zumrat slowed her steps. She could see the roof of her parents' house. She felt trapped. How could she get rid of him?

"Zumrat, you know I love you! I want to speak to your parents and get their permission to marry you!"

Walking faster again, Zumrat wanted to cover her ears with her hands. What could she do? Why was she so confused?

They reached her house and Zumrat entered her yard, Abdullah right behind her. He walked with her up to the front door.

"Yes! Okay. Yes!" The words leaped from her mouth.

"You will marry me?" Abdullah asked quietly as they heard footsteps inside the house on the wooden floor.

"Yes!" Zumrat looked up at his eager face. "Now you can leave! You don't need to ask!"

A wide smile spread over Abdullah's face. Joy sparkled in his deep brown eyes. "I will see you tomorrow!" In spite of trying to conceal his happiness, he was almost singing when he added, "Thank you, Zumrat!"

He walked backward down the path toward the street, beaming all over.

Zumrat smiled in return, but inside she was flustered. Whatever had come over her?

"But you told him you would marry him." The reproachful tones of the lady in their living room were tinged with perplexity. "Abdullah told me so just last night!" Their early morning visitor was clearly bewildered.

Sopia looked at her daughter. "Did you tell her son that you would marry him?"

Zumrat sighed, trying to figure out how to talk her way out of her predicament. Actually, she had been thinking about it the whole night long, tossing and turning on her bed. What had ever possessed her to say she would marry a man she was not even sure she liked?

"I said 'yes' to his question, but I did not mean 'yes' to marry him." Her answer did not make sense, even to her.

"I don't understand." Miryam was puzzled. "You said 'yes' but didn't mean 'yes'? Abdullah was all happy last evening when he told us he was going to be married. Now you say your 'yes' isn't a 'yes'?"

"That's right," Zumrat agreed. "I said 'yes,' but I didn't mean 'yes' to get married."

"Huh!" Sopia said in disgust. "Zumrat, you don't make any sense to anyone."

"I—I have to leave for work, or I will be late," Zumrat mumbled, glad to make her escape.

<hr />

"Let me try to explain," Zumrat told Abdullah earnestly that evening when he dutifully showed up to walk her home. Zumrat had tried to meet him with a smile, but all day she had been restless, and it was hard for her to see him again. "You see, last evening I said 'yes' because I did not want you to ask my parents if you could marry me. Don't you understand?"

Abdullah did not answer, but walked quietly beside her. The summer air felt hot and lifeless, and Zumrat tried to take deep breaths.

"You see, I don't think I am the one for you. You don't know me. I am not the person you are looking for. You don't need to try to win me. I'm not even sure I ever want to get married! I am a private person and I have my own feelings that I don't share with other people." The words just gushed out. "I want you to look for someone else. You don't know who I really am!"

Again Abdullah said nothing, just calmly walked beside her. Zumrat was irritated. Why didn't he talk? Why was he so silent? How could she make him understand how she felt?

Then, finally, her waiting ears heard him speak, not passionately, but simply and clearly. "My dear girl, I want to be the man who helps you understand yourself. I want to be someone you can talk to and learn to share your feelings with. I may not understand you now, but I am sure we can learn to know each other better. That is my position. I want to marry you because I love you."

He said nothing about his good position in the school where he was teaching or his prominence among his colleagues. Nor did he mention that he had money enough to support a wife and family. Abdullah spoke from his heart.

It was a time of soul searching for Zumrat. Her heart told her Abdullah seemed like a nice man, but another voice kept telling her she was not ready to commit herself. How could anyone else know her if she did not know herself?

This time when they reached her house, Sopia was standing at the front door watching for them. She took a good long look at the young man who wanted to marry her daughter, then turned and walked into the house without saying a word. Zumrat was amazed and turned toward Abdullah. He just smiled at her and said, "I will see you tomorrow."

When Zumrat entered the house, her mother was at work in the kitchen. Joining her, Zumrat got a glass and opened the spigot to get a drink.

"Well, I don't see that much in him myself! Many young men much better looking than him have tried to get your attention. I can see why you don't want him," Sopia said scornfully.

Zumrat froze with her empty glass halfway to the counter and looked at her mother in amazement. "What are you saying, Mother?"

Sopia raised her voice. "I said I don't see that much in him myself. Other young men much better looking than he have wanted to marry you. Why would you choose him?"

Setting her glass down slowly, Zumrat felt herself coming to

Abdullah's defense. "How can you say that? You don't know him. I mean, you don't know how he really is in his heart!" His recent words came to her in a rush.

. . . want to get to know you . . .

. . . learn to know each other . . .

She remembered with clarity how he was always respectful toward her and how he never spoke harshly or chattered on and on about himself like so many other young men did. She felt her heart grow warm with the memory of him.

Turning to face her mother squarely, Zumrat asked, "Who is going to live with him, me or you?"

"I thought you said this morning that you would not marry him! His mother left, shaking her head, and I told her it was no use if you had made up your mind." Sopia's voice rose in perplexity.

"I will marry him. I like him," Zumrat said with a smile. Just saying the words out loud reassured her that she was speaking from her heart. Yes, she did like him! She liked a lot of things about him! If she was going to marry, Abdullah was the one she would marry!

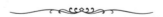

"Hey, Abdullah! What is this I hear?" Venyamin hurried up to his friend. "I hear you are getting married!"

"That's right," Abdullah said with a slow smile. "You heard right!"

"Now, let me get this straight. You are finally marrying, at the age of twenty-five! Well, well!" He grabbed Abdullah's arm. "Tell me, who's the lucky girl? Do I know her?"

"Her name is Zumrat," Abdullah replied eagerly, glad to share his news. "We are getting married next week."

"Zumrat?" Venyamin echoed. "The Zumrat I went to school

with? The Zumrat that was . . . well, the Zumrat everyone knew about at school?"

Abdullah shrugged his shoulders. "I guess. She's the only Zumrat I know."

There was a moment of silence, then Venyamin said slowly, "Are you sure, Abdullah, that you know what you are doing? How well do you know this girl?"

"Well enough that I want to marry her," Abdullah said with a grin. "And what I don't know, I am sure I will want to find out. Why?"

Venyamin shook his head. "We were all scared of her in school. I remember how she fought, even with the boys. She never let anyone get the best of her. I mean, she fought!"

Abdullah smiled again. "I believe you. She is a strong young lady. But I love her, and I want her for my wife. She is the one for me."

"Many others have wanted to marry her, but I could never forget my impression of her in school. I was too scared of her to ever approach her."

"Well, I am glad, Venyamin. That eliminated one more from her line of suitors. You made it easier for me!"

Venyamin clapped his hand on Abdullah's shoulder as they laughed together.

Chapter 3

"I get so frustrated!" Zumrat told her husband. "Every time I want to do something, like make a special meal for you, your mother wants to tell me exactly how I should make it. She says she knows better what you like than I do." Zumrat tried to talk calmly, but inside she was very upset.

"Be patient, dear." Abdullah stroked her hair. "I know my mother is a strong-minded woman, but . . ."

"Like me," Zumrat admitted. "But I can't stand to live in the same house with another strong-minded woman. I'm afraid sometime I'll say something I'll regret."

Clearing his throat, Abdullah said, "I have permission to build a house on my father's land. I was going to wait until I had enough money to build a big house, but maybe I should just go ahead and build a small one. Just for us."

Zumrat looked at him excitedly and placed her hand on his shoulder. "Oh, Abdullah, yes! Just a small one will do! It will be much better than living in this big house with your mother! I mean, I know it sounds awful, but you know, dear one, that your mother and I do not get along. Not at all!"

The six months since their wedding had gone by slowly for Zumrat. Right after the simple wedding ceremony at the state registrar's office, the young couple had moved into Abdullah's

Abdullah signs the marriage certificate at their simple wedding ceremony.

parents' house. At first, since they were both at their jobs during the day, everything had gone smoothly. Plus, it was early fall, and the newlyweds had spent their evenings in the park or walking around the city. But when the cold weather of early winter had come, they had spent more time indoors, and tension had begun to mount between the young wife and her mother-in-law.

"Yes!" Zumrat repeated. "Oh, please! When can you begin?"

"I love it when your eyes sparkle like that," Abdullah said, smiling at his bride. "You look so beautiful!"

Zumrat shook her head in mock exasperation. She blushed and got up to find paper and pencil. "Let's begin designing the house right away!"

"No need for any great designs," Abdullah warned her. "A simple two-roomed house will be all for now—just a kitchen and another room to sleep in. Later, I would like to build a big house for us."

"I don't care if it's small," Zumrat declared. "I still want to see it on paper. Look, here will be the front door, and here will be the windows. Oh, how long will it take?"

Abdullah said nothing, but he was smiling as they bent their heads over the paper and dreamed about their first home.

"Shush, shush!" Zumrat crooned to her firstborn. "Sleep now, dear son. I know it's noisy, but perhaps, just perhaps, they will go soon." She held baby Daniel close to her breast and rocked him back and forth in the tiny kitchen. A burst of noisy laughter came from the other room, where two of Abdullah's friends had joined him for the evening. The noise startled the baby, and he began to cry.

Just then Abdullah strode into the kitchen and asked, "Is the food ready yet?"

Zumrat glared at her husband. She said nothing, but shook her head curtly, looking meaningfully at her son.

"Well, they are asking for something to eat. As soon as you can, then." Abdullah turned and joined his comrades. Zumrat heard the clink of glasses as another round of vodka was poured.

She sighed and looked around her tiny kitchen. At first it had been so wonderful just to have a house by themselves that she had not minded the crowded conditions. Daniel had been born barely a year after they had been married, shortly after they had moved into their tiny house. Just to have her own house, her own kitchen, and her own husband had seemed so good to Zumrat that she had not minded the lack of space. But on evenings like this, when Abdullah's buddies came over and their party got loud and late, she wished for a quiet room for herself and her baby.

Daniel finally fell asleep. She carefully laid him in a box they had fixed for him and turned back to the stove. Abdullah always liked it when she cooked for his friends. She stirred the soup and checked the breadbox. At least there was plenty of bread.

Standing by the stove, Zumrat thought back to their brief courtship and marriage. A vague uneasiness ate at her. Had she done the right thing in getting married? Little niggling doubts crept into her mind. He had said he would help her understand herself. Had he? Was she any closer to understanding her own heart? Why was this emptiness still expanding inside her? Now they had their own house, and she no longer had to listen to her mother-in-law's nagging. She should be content. Her husband had a good salary, and his position as head of his department in school was prestigious. So what was missing?

Their plans to build a bigger house were materializing. They could expand. They would have room to entertain properly, not just some of Abdullah's drinking buddies. True, Abdullah never got drunk, but his friends got rather loud and seemed not to know when to leave.

"Anything to eat?" The loud voice from the doorway startled Zumrat.

"In a moment," she said rather sharply as she turned off the burner under the soup pot. But before she could finish, Daniel began crying again.

Zumrat hurried as fast as she could. She carried the soup bowls into the other room and set the small table. The baby's crying grew shriller, and in her haste she spilled some of the hot soup on her hand while she was pouring it into a bowl. Setting the bowl down, she ran cold water over her burn.

"Abdullah!" Zumrat called. "Would you come here?"

When he dutifully came, she said in a low voice. "I need to take care of Daniel. If you and your friends want to eat, you will have to take the food to them yourself." Then she turned to pick up her crying son.

At first Abdullah just stared at her. Then, wordlessly, he picked up the soup and carried it into the next room.

"Oh-ho! Look who's wearing the apron!" The men's blaring voices carried clearly into the kitchen. "She has you trained well already!"

In spite of her seething emotions, Zumrat tried to be gentle with her son as she drew him close. But Daniel seemed to sense his mother's frustration and wailed insistently.

Zumrat felt trapped. She wanted out. How, she had no idea, but unbidden thoughts crept into her weary mind. Oh, why had she ever married? The future stretched out in a long gray fog.

Abdullah sat at the little table staring dully at the plate in front of him. He heard Daniel's fretful cries from the kitchen, yet he did not move. His head ached and he felt so tired. Where was his breakfast?

"I can't for the life of me understand what is the matter with you." Zumrat's voice stirred him from his stupor. "You sit up all night long with your friends drinking vodka, then in the morning you can barely get up in time for work. I didn't marry you for this!"

Methodically, Abdullah took a piece of bread and spread it with butter. He didn't have enough energy to argue, especially so early in the morning.

Zumrat stared at her silent husband, then returned to the kitchen to pick up her wailing son. She shushed him and sat down on a chair to nurse him. The silence from the other room aggravated her.

"You don't answer when I speak to you." The words leaped from her mouth. "I cannot understand you! When we married, you told me you would help me understand myself, and now you don't even try to help me understand you!"

"Zumrat, they are my friends!" Abdullah protested, finally goaded into defending himself. "They come here because they like me! How can I tell them to leave?"

"Friends!" Zumrat snorted. "Some friends that keep us from going to bed like decent people! And while they are here, where are Daniel and I to rest? In the kitchen? That's where we spent most of last night!"

Quickly finishing his breakfast, Abdullah left for his job, more to get away from his wife's accusations than because it was time to leave. On the way to work, he stopped briefly to watch the construction of a new house. Masons were laying the brick walls, and as he watched their practiced moves, he felt a thrill come over him. These people were doing something that mattered! The men who were busily spreading mud and layering bricks were doing real work!

For the past several months, Abdullah had felt dissatisfied with his teaching job. He was tired of the staff's constant wrangling as they curried favor with the bosses and of the bribes to gain prestigious jobs within the Communist Party. Plus, he felt as though most of his students would much rather be elsewhere than in his classroom.

The next several days, Abdullah made sure he had ample time to watch the masons work. "I think I could do that," he told himself one evening.

Abdullah had more than one reason for wanting to change jobs. He was thinking more and more about building his own house—a big house right next to the small cottage they now lived in. Perhaps Zumrat would be happier then. With more room, his friends could still come, and his wife could go to another part of the house. Yes, it was time to make a change.

Chapter 4

"I have come back home to live," Zumrat told her mother as she stood on the doorstep of her old home with her baby son in her arms. "Abdullah insists on having his drinking friends at our tiny house, and I won't take it anymore."

"Ahh," Sopia said in a disgusted tone. "You never could get along with anyone. All during school you constantly got into fights. You fought me at home, and now you are fighting your husband. You will come to no good end!"

"Are you letting me in?" Zumrat ignored her mother's words.

"I will not be guilty of turning away my own flesh and blood," Sopia grumbled, stepping aside and holding the door open.

To Zumrat's surprise, it was her father who spoke seriously to her that evening when he came home from work.

"Listen," he said soberly, sitting down beside her on the sofa. "This is not a good idea."

Interrupting him, Zumrat said defiantly, "I can make my own living. I can go back to my old job and Daniel can stay at a baby care center. It might not be easy, but I can do it. I am strong enough."

"That's not what I meant," her father replied seriously. "You left Abdullah because you disagreed and had an argument with him. I tell you, you are making a big mistake. I have watched Abdullah since you were married, and such a husband is not easy to find. He provides well for you. He is not a drunkard." Lifting his hand to ward off her reply, he continued. "I know his friends come over to drink, but have you ever seen Abdullah drunk?"

Zumrat looked at the floor and shook her head.

Her father was not finished. "Good husbands are not easily found. You cannot go out to the market and find one. Even if you found a second husband, he would never be your real husband. And let me tell you something. Good wives make good husbands. You learn to be a good wife and see if Abdullah does not turn out to be a good husband."

Daniel stirred restlessly in her arms. Zumrat gazed at his tiny face.

"My advice is to swallow your pride and go back to him."

"I don't know if he wants me back," Zumrat admitted in a small voice. "I am afraid I hurt him deeply by leaving him."

The next several days, Zumrat tried to make herself at home with her parents again. She did not hear anything from her husband. By the time Abdullah came to beg her to return, Zumrat told him, "We'll see." She did not accompany her husband home that night.

However, living at home with her parents was not easy either. Her mother began throwing her faults at her and complaining about being burdened with a married daughter and her child. And Zumrat knew how her father felt about her running away from Abdullah. This hurt her deeply, for the bond between her and her father was still strong.

"I am giving notice of my resignation," Abdullah declared, facing his supervisor squarely. "I will be taking another job."

The elderly man looked in surprise at the serious, dark-haired man in front of him. "Taking another job?" he echoed. "You will never find another job as good as the one you have now. What's wrong? Why aren't you satisfied?"

With a slight shake of his head, Abdullah said nothing, but a small smile spread across his face. He was not going to tell his supervisor about all the petty wrangling among the staff to cut each other out and try to climb higher on the ladder of success. Abdullah knew he was already quite aware of it.

"I want to do something real—something I can see progress in."

"You must be crazy! You get 225 rubles a month with us! What can you do that is 'real' that will pay you that much?"

Abdullah leaned forward. "I am confident that soon I will be making twice what I make here. Plus, I will be doing something I like."

For a moment the older man was silent, then he shrugged. "Okay. I accept your resignation. Put it into writing and clear out your desk. There are plenty of people who want your job. It's nothing to me."

So Abdullah began work with the masons. He learned quickly and enjoyed it. His dream of building a house with his own hands was coming within reach. Perhaps he could persuade Zumrat to return to him after she saw the house he was building for her. For them.

Abdullah paused outside his little house one evening after coming home from work. It sounded as though someone was inside. Yes, someone was in the kitchen! He pushed the door open.

"Uh . . . hi." Zumrat looked up from her work by the stove.

Abdullah stood hesitantly on the doorstep. He saw Daniel sitting on the floor, playing with his toys.

"You're back," he said at last, somewhat awkwardly. He hardly knew what to say or what she expected him to do.

"Yes, if you will have me," Zumrat replied, not meeting his eyes.

"I missed you," he stated simply. "I want you here with me." Then he walked over to their son and squatted down beside him. The little boy looked up at his daddy and smiled. Abdullah picked him up.

Zumrat came over to her husband, and he slipped his arm around her waist. Her smile was rather timid, but to Abdullah it was as warming as the sun on a cold day.

"Come inside and warm up," Alexander invited, nodding toward his house and beckoning to Abdullah. "It's still a long way to your home, and I'm sure Maria will have something hot for you to drink."

Abdullah hesitated for a moment. Another gust of icy air swirled the snow around the two.

He had learned much during his first several months as a mason. One day while he was walking home, he had noticed Alexander's crew building a house. He had been intrigued by the interesting way Alexander laid the bricks above the windows and between the first and second stories.

"I would like to work for you and learn how to do that," he had told Alexander. And that's how his friendship with Alexander had started.

Alexander bent his head into the wind and headed for the front door. "Well, I'm getting out of this. Come on!" Abdullah followed.

The two stamped the snow from their boots as they stood in the enclosed front entrance. The door to the house opened, and a cheerful, beaming face greeted the two men.

"Maria, do you have something warm for Abdullah to drink before he goes home in this wind?" Alexander asked with a smile.

"Why, yes! Come in! You must be almost frozen! I can't see how you could even work today."

"We worked all morning until the wind started picking up," Alexander replied. "That's why we quit early." He turned to Abdullah. "Maria, this is my new worker, Abdullah. He told me he's just learning, but he's already laying bricks, and doing it well."

"I'm glad to meet you," Maria said warmly. "I'm glad Alexander has found good help."

Maria hurried out to the kitchen and Alexander motioned to a chair. "Sit down by the radiator and warm yourself."

The large room was comfortably furnished. Big windows with potted plants faced the street.

"Did you build this house yourself?" Abdullah asked.

"My wife and I did," Alexander laughed as Maria hurried in with steaming cups of tea. "Didn't we?" He looked at her and they both laughed.

"You did, dear," she said with a chuckle. "I just told you what I wanted, and you did it."

"Oh, you did much more than that. You drew up the plans and pitched in during the building." Turning to Abdullah, who was taking the first sip of the fragrant tea, he said, "I never had to clean up. Maria always kept all the trash and junk cleaned right up. She's quite a worker!"

Maria blushed at her husband's praise. "Will you have more tea?" she asked as soon as Abdullah's cup was half empty.

He stretched out his arm, and she refilled the cup from the

teapot. Her face was wreathed in smiles, and little crinkles beside her eyes gave her a merry look.

"I must go," Abdullah said when he had emptied his second cup. "My wife will have supper waiting for me." Reluctantly he left the warm, cheerful house and braved the elements again.

He knew he shouldn't, but he couldn't help but contrast Maria with his own wife. Zumrat often seemed preoccupied and somewhat glum in the evenings. She seemed a little more settled since her return, and he knew she was trying to make their home a happy one, but she was not cheerful and often complained about life.

Not like Maria. The vision of that cheerful, smiling face floated before Abdullah's eyes. So friendly! So . . . how could he say? Not in the least flirtatious, but just . . . happy, somehow. Joyful! That was the word. So joyful!

Was it Alexander who made her that way?

Abdullah had already worked long enough with his boss to know that Alexander was no saint. Sure, he was nice enough as a boss and not hard to get along with, but really, he was just another man. Maria's happiness must come from somewhere else.

"You are home early," Zumrat said when he stepped inside his home. "I hope you don't expect supper right away. I had no idea you would be home so soon."

"That's all right," Abdullah answered softly. "What did you do today?"

Zumrat looked at him sharply. What was her husband up to? "Just the usual things. I took care of Daniel and went to the market. Why do you ask?"

Flushing slightly, Abdullah shrugged his shoulders and said nothing. It would have been hard for him to explain why he had asked, even to himself.

With a sigh Zumrat turned back to her work. She did not understand her husband. Why was he strange like this all at once? Usually so quiet and uncommunicative, now all at once asking her what she had done that day. She did not care in the least what he did at his work.

Chapter 5

"Now, Zumrat, the next time you come you must bring me some of your bread!" Maria said sincerely as she helped her new friend bundle little Daniel for the journey home.

"Oh, I'm sure you can bake better bread than I can," Zumrat replied somewhat shyly. She was not used to sharing openly. However, though this was their first meeting, she already felt more at home with Maria than with people she had known for a long time.

"I'm always looking for another kind of bread. You know how we women are," Maria's laugh bubbled over again, "always looking for another recipe to try!"

Zumrat smiled in response. "I will bring you some," she said as she put on her coat.

"I can't tell you how much it meant for you to call on me today," Maria said seriously. "I'm still not over my morning sickness, and even though I know it's nothing serious, there are days when I just don't want to get out of bed."

"I know the feeling," Zumrat said softly, smoothing her coat over her own bulging stomach. She picked up Daniel, all wrapped up in his winter clothes, and grunted slightly. "He's getting so heavy!"

"You will soon need a baby stroller," Maria said. "When you have two, that will help a lot."

After saying goodbye, Zumrat went on her way. Maria waved from her front door as Zumrat hurried out the walk on the way to the bus.

"I went today," Zumrat told Abdullah that evening during supper.

Abdullah sipped the soup from his spoon. "Went where?" he asked, wiping his mouth.

Zumrat stared at him. Why was he so dull? Why didn't he ever know what she was talking about? Were all men so slow-witted? "To Maria! I thought you would know! You've been telling me I should go see your friend's wife, and now when I tell you I went, you ask where I went!"

Abdullah bent over his soup bowl and finished the hot soup. "I'm glad," he said simply. "She will be good for you."

Abruptly, Zumrat got up from the table. He wasn't even interested in how her visit went! He was just glad she had done what he had suggested! She shook her head. There just wasn't any sense in trying to figure him out.

"Will you go again?" Abdullah wanted to know.

Shrugging one shoulder, Zumrat began to clear the table. "I don't know," she said shortly. "It's not as though we know each other."

Once more silence filled the room, broken only by Daniel's childish chatter.

As Zumrat washed the dishes, she felt her cheeks flush in shame. She really did plan to go see Maria again. Something in Maria's cheerful presence made her want to know her better.

She just hadn't wanted to acknowledge to Abdullah that his suggestion to become acquainted with Maria interested her. She scrubbed the soup pot vigorously as tears pricked her eyelids. She sniffed and tried to control her thoughts.

***

"I have had enough!" Zumrat burst out with passion. "I'm leaving Abdullah! We argue constantly and he never seems to understand me!"

"Come, come." Maria did not seem at all alarmed at the outburst. She took Daniel from Zumrat's arms and led the distraught mother to a comfortable chair. "There, there." She patted Zumrat's arm and put Daniel in her lap. "I'll bring in the tea, then you can tell me all about it."

Zumrat sighed and began to unbutton her son's coat. She looked around the peaceful room.

Was this her tenth visit? Her eleventh? She wasn't sure. As the weeks had stretched into months, the two women had become fast friends. Sometimes Maria visited their house, but usually Zumrat went to see Maria. "Your house is so much nicer—and bigger," she would tell her friend, though she knew Abdullah was trying to please her by putting as much time as he could into building their house. He was already halfway finished.

"Here, let me take Daniel. My, you are growing into a young man already!" Maria chucked the little boy under his chin. He responded with a big grin.

"I'm sorry I burst in on you like this," Zumrat said, sipping the fragrant tea. "I feel all bunched up inside, and I just don't think I can go on living with Abdullah. We just don't understand each other. Yet I don't want to leave him either. I still love him, but why do his actions, or lack of them, aggravate me so?"

"You are too distraught to make a decision right now," Maria told her gently. "You tried living separately before and it didn't work. Don't be hasty in leaving your husband."

Zumrat sipped her tea again. Outside the wind was still blowing, even though spring was already tempering the cold. She felt her baby move inside her.

As though reading her thoughts, Maria said, "You will soon have another child. Is this the time to consider leaving your husband?"

Zumrat's tea splattered as she set her cup forcefully back on the saucer. "I just feel so torn up inside. So . . . I don't know how to say it." Tears seeped out of the corners of her dark eyes.

"I know someone who can help you," Maria said, feeling the Holy Spirit prompt her to speak.

"Who is that?" Zumrat asked in a disbelieving tone.

"Jesus!"

The word filled the room. Zumrat stared at Maria. Then she found her voice. "Jesus? That's your god, not mine!"

This was not the first time Maria had spoken about Jesus. In fact, she spoke so openly and freely about Jesus that Zumrat almost expected to find him somewhere in Maria's house. He seemed as close to her as a friend.

"Jesus is not just my God. He will be God to anyone who trusts in Him."

"But we are Muslims! You know that!" Even to her own ears, her words sounded ridiculous. She knew she was not a Muslim. Her grandmother might have lit candles and recited prayers, but nothing like that was ever done in her parents' home. Still, her heritage was Muslim, even if her faith wasn't.

It was different for Abdullah. His grandparents had been deeply religious and had tried to raise their children to respect and honor Mohammed, so their Muslim heritage was much more important to Abdullah than to her. Zumrat had never been at all religious and prided herself on being a product of the modern generation. She had never even considered becoming a Christian. Now Maria said this Jesus, this Christian man, could help her. How could this be possible?

"I don't know anything about Jesus! How could he help me, a woman with a little child and a baby on the way?" Zumrat looked at her friend in total amazement.

"Do you want to hear how Jesus can help you? Do you want to know who Jesus is?" Maria asked gently, sensing curiosity in Zumrat's tone.

For the next hour, Maria told Zumrat about the life of Jesus, explaining to her just why Jesus came into the world and what he could do for those who accepted him into their hearts.

"It's a wonderful story," Zumrat said as she prepared to leave. "But that Jesus could help my marriage is beyond me! How could this story, even if it is true, have any effect on my life? This is 1985, and you say he lived 2,000 years ago!"

Maria smiled and gave her an affectionate hug. "But remember, I told you He rose from the grave and is alive today! That's why He can help you."

"Does Alexander believe this too?" Zumrat asked.

With a brave smile, Maria said, "Not yet. But I have faith that someday he will."

Shaking her head, Zumrat left. It was all too strange. But that evening when she and Abdullah had another argument over some trivial matter, Zumrat remembered Maria's words. "I know someone who can help you. Jesus!" For some reason, those words kept ringing in her ears.

"Nothing has changed," Zumrat said dully. "We still argue. He still doesn't understand my needs, and sometimes he just won't talk. I don't think I can stay with him any longer."

Kneeling beside her friend, Maria said sincerely, "Will you pray with me?"

"I don't know how to pray," Zumrat said, looking with clouded eyes at her friend.

"I will teach you," Maria said, pulling her down on the floor beside her.

The two women were alone, for Zumrat had left Daniel with her married sister. She had come once more to Maria's house to vent her frustration, determined this time to move back in with her parents. Life was just too difficult with Abdullah. Life was too difficult any way she looked at it.

"Dear Jesus," Maria said, closing her eyes, "we need your help!"

At first, Zumrat said nothing, then she repeated Maria's words. "Dear Jesus, we need your help."

Sentence by sentence, Maria led Zumrat through her first prayer—nothing fancy, just simple words, like one friend talking to another.

Zumrat stumbled through the prayer. It felt strange to talk to someone she couldn't see. Maria had told her that Jesus could hear her. She had said he could hear the language of her heart— her deep, innermost feelings. She had said he even knew the words Zumrat could not express.

It was a strange feeling, this praying. Zumrat peeked at her friend.

Maria was weeping! She was crying for her, Zumrat! It made tears come to her own eyes. She felt them streaming down her face. It was a strange experience to let herself cry. She had always forced her tears back.

She heard Maria softly whispering words in her prayer. She listened closely, but she did not know what Maria was saying. It sounded like another language—a heavenly language.

"I feel different," Zumrat said in surprise when they got up after prayer. "I don't know why, but I feel . . . not so heavy."

Maria nodded in understanding. "When you tell Jesus about your troubles and your heartaches, He takes them away from you. He wants to carry your troubles."

"It's a strange feeling," Zumrat said in awe. "I don't know how to talk about it."

The strangeness lasted. That evening, Abdullah's habits were not as annoying to her. When he seemed at a loss to understand what she was talking about, it no longer irked her to have to explain. She found herself telling him all kinds of things about her life, and he listened appreciatively. They talked about the house he was building for them and about the approaching birth of their second child.

Throughout that evening Zumrat was aware that her husband was studying her keenly. He almost seemed puzzled. But his long, silent looks did not bother her as they used to. She found herself talking about anything.

But she did not mention her strange experience with Maria. She did not even tell him about going to visit her friend. If she did, she might find herself telling him that she had gone with intentions of leaving their home again. She did not want to reveal that. Not this evening.

Chapter 6

Abdullah washed his hands in the sink and dried them on the towel. He straightened his back and stretched his arms upward. Looking around the back entry, he felt a glow of satisfaction. He really liked their new house.

It had taken a while to get it finished, but he had worked long and hard, and now they had been living in this much bigger and better house for two months.

He looked through the glass window into the kitchen. He could not see Zumrat and figured she must be with the children. Perhaps she was taking care of their little girl, Dilnoza, or checking on Daniel, making sure he was sleeping well.

It had been a good summer. Not only had he been able to finish their house, work had gone well also. And there was something else. He could hardly place his finger on it, yet Abdullah was sure something had happened.

Placing the towel back on the rack, Abdullah pondered the change. What had made their home more peaceful than ever before?

Smiling, he pushed open the door into the kitchen

Abdullah and Zumrat's house in Osh

and glanced at the clean countertops. Zumrat was a stickler for neatness. Even with two small children, she always found time to keep their house clean and tidy. She worked efficiently, and her husband rarely came home to a messy house.

Running his hand over the tile countertop, Abdullah's thoughts returned to his earlier ruminating. What was it that made life different? Was Zumrat happier now that they finally had more room? Even though his drinking buddies still came over and stayed late, she no longer complained about it. True, she did not have to be bothered by the noise anymore, but was it just that? Did having her own room mean that much to her? Abdullah was not sure it was only the big house that made her more . . . well, more like Maria.

It had been a good suggestion to have his wife get to know his boss's wife. Zumrat and Maria had become good friends. He knew, and never minded, that the two women spent much time together. At times when he came home from work Zumrat and the children were gone, but there was always a note, and most of the time his supper was waiting for him.

Now where was his wife? Abdullah went through the big living room and crossed through the front hall, walking softly. Even though it was late in the evening, the twilight still illuminated the house, making electric lights unnecessary.

There she was, sitting in a rocking chair by the window, reading. Abdullah paused for a moment, thinking what a nice picture she made, reading intently, sitting quietly for once. The children must both be sleeping.

"What are you reading?" he asked softly. He did not want to wake the children.

Zumrat jumped slightly. "Oh! I didn't hear you come in! You were very quiet." She got up and they went into the living room.

Even though the house was not completely furnished, they had a nice couch and several soft chairs. Abdullah noticed that Zumrat still carried her book, although she let her hand hang by her side, partially hiding it.

He snapped on a reading lamp and asked again, "What were you reading when I came in? You were so absorbed that you never heard me coming to the door."

Was his wife blushing? Zumrat did not say anything right away and turned slightly away from him.

"Here, let me see." Abdullah walked up to her and held out his hand.

"Maria gave it to me to read," Zumrat said, handing the book to her husband.

Moving over to the sofa, Abdullah held it up to the light. "It's a Christian book!" he said, looking at the text. "It's an Old Slavonic New Testament! Right here it says so!" Abdullah pointed to the title on the worn cover.

"Yes," Zumrat said. "I am finding it interesting. Even though it's not in Russian, I find I can understand the old Slavic language."

"Why would you waste your time reading from an antique book about Christians? You never seemed interested in history before. Plus, it's written in Old Slavonic! We hardly ever read anything but Russian anymore." Abdullah opened the pages and began skimming the words. "We don't need teachings about Jesus in this house."

Zumrat did not answer as he continued to turn the pages. "Where did Maria get this book?" he asked.

"She had it in her house. One day she asked if I would like to read it, and I said I would, so she let me borrow it."

Her husband had stopped flipping pages and was reading. Zumrat waited silently. She took a deep, slow breath. Abdullah frowned. He turned the page and kept reading. Then, suddenly, he snapped the book shut. Zumrat jumped at his sudden movement. She felt his eyes on her face.

"Give it back," he said firmly. "We don't need any Christian stuff in our house. We are from the new generation."

"Yes, I will give it back," Zumrat said quickly. "It's just borrowed."

Two days later, she was reading it again.

"I thought I told you to return that book." Abdullah's voice rose in frustration. "Now you are reading it again! Why are you so interested in something that should not be in our house? It should not be in our country! We don't need dead men's ideas! We are a new society, headed for greatness!" The Soviets had indoctrinated their youth well, and Abdullah thought of himself as a realist who did not need religion for a crutch—especially not a foreign religion like Christianity. Did they not have their own religion? True, hardly anyone except the elderly attended prayers at the mosques, but every time the call for prayer sounded from the minarets, the faithful spread out their prayer rugs and bowed toward Mecca, their holy city, and prayed. Abdullah hardly ever prayed anymore, but he remembered his visits with his grandparents, and his grandfather had always insisted the young boy join him in his prayers.

But he had finished with all that long ago. No religion for him now!

So when he caught his wife for the third time reading from the New Testament several days later, something snapped inside him.

"Zumrat!" Abdullah yelled in a tone that surprised even himself. "I have told you twice to take that book back to Maria! Now you're reading it again! Whatever has gotten into you?"

Zumrat looked up, her eyes defiant. Then, bowing her head, she said calmly, "I will give it back, but I just haven't done it yet. There is so much more I want to read. I want to know more about . . ."

"About what?" Abdullah shouted. His loud voice startled the baby in Zumrat's arms and Dilnoza began to cry.

"About what is written. It helps me," Zumrat said, rocking the infant back and forth in her arms, the book on her lap.

Abdullah grabbed the book. Reaching up, Zumrat exclaimed, "Oh, don't ruin it! It's not mine! I will give it back!"

"No Christian books in my house!" Abdullah's rage boiled over. He could not tell why this book upset him so much, but there was something strange going on in his house, and this book had something to do with it.

"I am going to tear it up! I don't care if it is borrowed! The world will be better off without such a book anyway!" He opened the book and bent the spine backward.

"Oh, please!" Zumrat sprang out of her chair with a cry. "Just give it back, and I promise I will return it to Maria! I can take it tomorrow morning, first thing!" Her voice rose in alarm as she watched her husband rip the book apart. The baby's cries grew louder.

When the pages fluttered to the floor, Zumrat knelt in

anguish in front of her husband. "Oh, please, don't do this! You don't know what you are doing! Oh, you will be punished for destroying this book!"

Abdullah heard her through his rage. He flung the remaining pages onto the floor and let the cover fall. It thudded dully on the wooden boards.

Zumrat carried the wailing baby from the room, but before she left, Abdullah saw that her cheeks were wet. She was crying! Over a book!

Deeply disturbed, Abdullah went to bed. He heard his wife in the living room, taking care of the baby. He lay in the dark, wide awake, trying to think. He could see the pages of the book through the open door. Then, as he watched, he saw Zumrat quietly gather up the torn book. She handled the pages gently, pressing them flat again.

With a bound, he was up. He grabbed the pages from his wife and carried them to the outhouse in the yard. Opening the lid, he pushed them through the hole and dropped them in. Now see if she would try to rescue them!

When he went back to their bedroom, breathing heavily, Zumrat was lying silently on her side of the bed. Abdullah lay down and tried to relax. Zumrat did not move.

About thirty minutes later the bed moved slightly. Abdullah pretended he was sleeping, and when Zumrat quietly got up and left the room, he waited several seconds before he got up and listened to her footsteps go through the living room and into the kitchen. He heard the click of the lock on the back door, then it closed gently.

By the time Abdullah was out the back door, he saw a flashlight inside the outhouse. He crept up and peeped through a crack in the door. Zumrat had already fished a number of pages out of the hole. She was still going to try to save as much of that book as she could!

He waited until she had stacked the pages on the floor, then flung open the door and grabbed them. This time she was not going to rescue that book! The fire in the trash pit still had hot ashes. Stalking away from his startled wife, Abdullah flung the pages into the pit. Poking them with a stick, Abdullah felt a glow of triumph as the hot ashes ignited the paper and tongues of fire leaped upward.

"Oh, Abdullah! Don't destroy those words! This is not good!" He heard despair in her voice, but something drove him on.

"Now they are gone forever!" Abdullah retorted. "Christian books will no longer plague our house! Let that be a lesson to you!"

Zumrat said nothing as she watched the flames lick the edges of the pages. She could nearly read the words as the bright firelight illuminated them before consuming them. Suddenly, with a shrill cry, she reached into the fire and tried to snatch the papers from the flames.

"You're crazy, Zumrat! You will burn yourself!" Abdullah grabbed his wife and pulled her away. "What is the matter with you?"

Zumrat was shaking with sobs. She leaned her head against her husband's chest and cried, "Oh, what is going to happen to you? Surely you will be punished!"

"What are you talking about? Nothing will happen to me! Why do you keep saying that? It's just a book!" A note of uncertainty crept into his voice. Was there something special about this book? Why would anyone go through all his wife had gone through just to rescue some old pages from a history book? What was going on? "Come inside and wash up. It's late, and we need to go to bed. The neighbors will wonder what's happening. They will think we are fighting."

Obediently, Zumrat allowed him to lead her back to the house. After they had washed and were lying in bed, Abdullah could not sleep. His mind worked busily, trying to make sense of all that had happened.

Why had he become so upset about that book? He knew about religion. What had made him react so violently tonight?

His sleepless thoughts drifted back to his childhood. He remembered how, night after night, he had felt there was something in his room. Not something—someone. He remembered a night he had been sure he had seen a pair of eyes watching him in the dark. He had not been scared, but rather interested. Were they the eyes of God? His grandfather had often told him stories about the patriarchs and how God had appeared to people back then. Was God coming to him, a young boy in Kyrgyzstan in the city of Osh? Was that possible?

Abdullah had not known then, and had thought he had put all those things behind him. As a grown man, he still did not know, but now he wondered anew. What was there to religion? Why did some people take religion so seriously, while others, like himself, had few religious thoughts? What did Zumrat believe? He was sure she'd had no interest in religion when they had married. In fact, she had seemed less interested in religion than he had been. Now why was she all at once so interested in a Christian book?

He tossed restlessly. Beside him, Zumrat lay still. Was she sleeping? He did not know.

Something had happened in their home. Before, he had understood that the tension between them was his fault. His habits, like staying up late when his friends came over, had frustrated Zumrat. But he had always told himself that all wives were like that. He had heard his friends' wives nagging at their husbands, wanting this, wanting that, always discontent with their lots in life. That was what all wives did.

Except Alexander's wife. She was different. Not once had he heard her complain to her husband. She was always so cheerful, so hospitable. Yes, there was definitely something different about Maria.

That was what was happening. Zumrat was becoming more like Maria! The thought jolted him. Things hadn't changed all at once—just little changes here and there. She had stopped fussing at him, for one. Her voice had changed too. She no longer whined and complained as she had in the past. Yes, something was changing in his wife.

What was it? Could it possibly be connected to the book she had been reading? Why had Zumrat so desperately wanted to save those pages? An uneasy feeling hounded the sleepless man, and his head reeled from too many questions. He had thought his life was settling into a nice, regular pattern, but now something strange was happening to him. To them.

Outside the open window a car passed, then all was quiet again. A dog barked somewhere in the distance, and Abdullah wished it would shut up. He felt tense. He desperately wanted to sleep, but sleep was far away.

All through the long night he tossed and turned, sometimes drifting into a restless sleep. He was wide awake when Dilnoza cried, and he was awake the whole time Zumrat held their tiny daughter.

In the morning he did not want to get up and face another day. His head ached and he felt like an old man. He knew he was grouchy with Zumrat and the children, and when he finally left for work, he seemed to have no energy. He had no idea what had come over him, but he felt terrible, just terrible.

Chapter 7

"Sure, I'll come and help," Abdullah told his friend. "My work can wait, or my masons can go on without me. After all, you're the one who set me on my feet in this business. In fact, it's been over a year since you encouraged me to start my own crew."

Alexander laughed. "I think you set your own pace on how fast you learned to lay brick! Have you ever wished you had stayed in that school where you used to teach? I mean, many people enjoy jobs like that. No warm weather to sweat through during the summer and no cold winter weather to make you wish you were inside."

Shaking his head, Abdullah replied, "No, I have never regretted giving up that job. Constant bickering and cutting each other out . . . Those years and the years I spent in the army were enough to convince me that bureaucratic jobs are not for me!"

He laughed, and when Alexander asked what was funny, he said, "I remember my boss telling me I couldn't find a job that would pay as well as teaching. Well, I could go to him now and tell him I am making more than twice as much money as I used to make!"

"There will always be work for masons," Alexander agreed. "You have done well. You've built your own house and have prospered over the years I have known you."

"What are you working on now?" Abdullah asked. "What will you need help with?"

"A restaurant," Alexander told him. "This will be a big job, and I want to get it done as quickly as I can. Thanks for offering to help. It means a lot to me."

"Sure." Abdullah paused, considering if this was the right time to bring up the subject that had been weighing on his mind. He started in hesitantly. "By the way, ever since Zumrat has been going over to your house to see Maria, she is different."

"How is she different?" Alexander asked, pushing his shovel into the ground and placing one foot on the edge.

"Well," Abdullah hesitated, "she's just kinder. She hardly ever complains anymore."

"I know what you mean," Alexander said. "Maria used to whine and complain all the time, but in the last three years she has changed drastically."

"Maria?" Abdullah pulled his eyebrows together. "I can never imagine her complaining or fussing."

"Ho-ho! You didn't know her soon after we got married. Back then, she didn't even want children. Now we have Arnold, and she can't give him enough love! I tease her and tell her she loves that little boy more than she loves me, but I know it's not true, and I never have to worry. Our marriage has never been better."

The two men were silent for a moment. Then Abdullah said, "That is strange. I wonder what made them change."

"I can tell you. After Maria began to listen to Heinrich, she began to change. Now I notice a change whenever she attends one of the meetings."

"Meetings? Heinrich?" Abdullah was puzzled.

"Yep. That Heinrich fellow came here to Osh and began

meeting with several people, mostly women, and after Maria started going, I could tell something had happened to her. Something good."

Suddenly Alexander pulled the shovel from the ground. "Here we are, talking like a couple of women when there is work to be done. It will be like old times, working together again!" He slapped his friend jovially on the shoulder, and they turned and walked off together.

"I know someone who can heal Sherzat," Zumrat told her sister earnestly.

"Who?" Sofia asked despondently, holding her six-month-old son. The two sisters looked at the frail child in Sofia's lap. They were both thinking of the two infants Sofia had lost before Sherzat was born. Both had died before they reached their first birthday. Now Sherzat was sick.

"Jesus can heal him," Zumrat said simply.

"Jesus?" Sofia said with a sharp intake of breath. "What does a Christian god have to do with healing my son?"

"I have read it in the New Testament," Zumrat told her. "He not only healed the sick, he raised the dead!"

"Well, I tell you, if Jesus heals my son, I will believe in Him." She looked at her listless child and then up at Zumrat. "Where did you learn about Jesus? What have you been reading?"

"One of my friends gave me a New Testament to read," Zumrat said slowly. She did not want to tell her sister what had happened to it. "I read about the miracles Jesus did, and I read that if we have faith and believe, He will do those things for us too."

"Who is this friend who gave you this book?"

"Her name is Maria. I have learned a lot from her."

Looking at her son, Sofia said, "I want my son to live. I want to have a healthy child."

Zumrat made a sudden decision. "I will take you to Heinrich. He will pray for Sherzat."

"I can't take him outside. He has a high fever." Sofia laid her hand on her son's hot forehead. "I must take him to the hospital."

"No, no!" Zumrat objected. "You took the others to the hospital, and they died! Come, we will take a taxi. I will pay."

The bewildered mother found herself hustled into a taxi, clutching her sick son in her arms.

"What will this man say?" Sofia wondered as they drove through the city. "He doesn't even know me!"

"He will be glad to see you," Zumrat assured her sister. "He welcomes everyone."

As they climbed the apartment stairs, Sofia felt uneasiness creep over her. How could Zumrat be so sure that this Heinrich could help her? But no, she had said Jesus could heal Sherzat. She felt confused.

"Come in, come in!" Zina, Heinrich's wife, welcomed them when she answered the doorbell.

"This is my sister," Zumrat told the couple when Heinrich came to see who had arrived. "Sofia has had two babies who died before they were a year old. Now Sherzat is sick with a fever. I told her Jesus could heal him."

"Come into the living room," Heinrich invited, leading the way. "Take chairs. Yes, Jesus can heal the sick. He is the living Lord!"

"I read in the New Testament that Jesus did miracles. He said if we have faith and believe, He will answer our prayers. I want Sofia to know that Jesus can heal her son. Will you pray for Sherzat?" Zumrat asked simply.

"Yes! Come, let us kneel and pray," Heinrich answered instantly.

Sofia knelt on the floor beside the others. She held her son close. She listened as Heinrich prayed. She heard him talking to Jesus as though He was right in the room. As she listened, tears began rolling down her cheeks. A feeling she had never experienced before swept over her. Yes, she could feel a vibrant presence in the room with them!

Then she heard her sister and Zina praying. All three of them were praying at the same time. At times she could pick out different phrases, and other times she could not understand.

Sofia had never prayed before. She did not know how to pray. But as she wept softly, something broke in her heart and she found herself saying, "Oh, please, heal my son!"

How much later, Sofia did not know, but when she felt Sherzat's forehead, it was cool to her touch. She looked intently at her son as he lay in her arms, breathing quietly. He was better!

"He is better!" Her voice broke into the prayers of the others. "His fever is gone!"

With joy, the little group lifted their hands and praised Jesus, the Healer. All of them together rejoiced in the power of their Lord. Jesus had heard their prayers.

Sofia called Zumrat the next morning. "He slept all night. He seems much better, and he drinks his milk. Jesus did something wonderful to my son!"

The group of believers that met regularly was growing. Now Sofia accompanied her sister to the meetings and eagerly drank in the Gospel. "Yes, I believe in Jesus!" she told the group one day. "He healed my son! I know he is God!"

With joy, Heinrich led the weeping woman in prayer as she repented of her sins and made a declaration of her faith in Christ. Zumrat and the other women embraced her happily.

"Did you repent too?" Sofia asked as the two left Maria's house, where the believers met.

"I did," Zumrat replied. "Before Dilnoza was born, I realized I was a sinner, so I repented and asked Jesus to come into my life. Since then I have been learning more and more about how to live the way Jesus wants me to live."

"How did you learn?"

"I try to attend the meetings Heinrich schedules for those who want to know more about the Christian life. And I read the New Testament."

"The New Testament! Where can I get one?" Sofia asked eagerly.

"The one we had was destroyed. We are praying for another one. Heinrich has one that he shares, but we are asking God for another one so we can take turns reading it in our homes." She did not want to tell her sad tale to her sister. She had already told Maria, and the two women had wept over their loss.

"Oh, I wish I could have one to read! Wouldn't it be wonderful if we could each have our own?"

The two walked together in silence, then Sofia asked, "Do our relatives know that you are a Christian?"

The tapping of their heels on the sidewalk sounded loud to Zumrat. "I told Mother," she said finally.

"And?" Sofia asked.

"She told me that if Abdullah throws me out—and she let me know that he would have every right to do so—I was not to come back to her house, for she would no longer let me live there." Zumrat sobered at the memory of her mother's wrath.

"I didn't know our parents were religious," Sofia observed, puzzled. "They never taught us to be."

Zumrat nodded. "I think our people just get very upset and suddenly become religious whenever the name of Jesus is mentioned. Very upset," she repeated as she remembered Abdullah's anger over the New Testament.

"Does Abdullah know you are a Christian?"

"I have not told him. He got extremely angry when he discovered me reading the New Testament, and I have not been brave enough to tell him. I am trying to let him know by my life."

"You have changed," Sofia told her. "You don't seem so angry anymore. Not like I remember you used to be when we were all at home."

"I was angry. I didn't know why, but now I know I was looking for answers to my questions about life. When I became a Christian, that empty feeling inside me was gone. I now have a purpose for my life—living for my Lord!"

The two sisters, young in their faith but wise in their experiences with Christ, rejoiced in their new bond as believers in Jesus.

"Thank you for telling me about Jesus," Sofia said with joy. "I wanted healing for Sherzat, and He did that, but He also healed my heart!"

Abdullah ducked to pass under the grape arbor in the backyard where they were building the restaurant. The load in the brick carrier was heavy. Thinking he had cleared the low tunnel, he stood up to relieve his tired back, but as he straightened, his head hit the metal channel that held up the corner of the arbor. The steel piece was not fastened to the wood, and his head pushed it up. As Abdullah ducked from the blow, the metal channel fell on his head.

Abdullah let the bricks fall to the ground and collapsed on top of them with a groan. Immediately he put his hand to his head and felt blood seeping through his hair.

"Are you all right?" Through his pain, Abdullah heard a man's voice above him.

He could not answer, for he felt dizzy and nauseated. The man lifted him to a sitting position. "Let me get something for your head. You are bleeding!"

Abdullah knew his head was cut open, for he could feel the blood seeping into his shirt collar, but he didn't know how deep the cut was. The man bound his head, and Abdullah tried to get up.

"You must go to the hospital." The man was alarmed at the amount of blood that had oozed out of the wound. He kept dabbing at it with another piece of material.

"Help me clean up so I can go home," Abdullah said after a while. "I don't want to go to the hospital. I will go home."

Despite the protests of the man who had come to his aid, Abdullah carefully put on his cap and, holding onto the sides of buildings, made it to the bus stop. Several times on the bus he thought he would faint, but somehow he made it home.

"Zumrat! Come help me!" he called as soon as he entered their home. Pain shot through his head and he had difficulty seeing.

Zumrat rushed into the hall and caught him as he swayed. "What happened? Come, you must sit down! Oh, your head! It's bleeding!"

She steered him to the bed and Abdullah sat on the edge. When Zumrat took his cap off, she gasped. "Oh, Abdullah! You should not have done that!" Then she clapped her hand over her mouth and began to cry.

"Please, get some water and wash the blood away," Abdullah said. "Why are you crying?"

"You are being punished for what you did!" The words leaped out of Zumrat's mouth. "Oh, God, help us!"

The book! Zumrat thought he was being punished because he had destroyed that book! In spite of his pain, Abdullah remembered.

"Please, help me! Get some water and wash my head. I want to lie down," Abdullah pleaded. The room began to spin in a dizzying circle.

Immediately Zumrat left and came back with a bowl of water. As she gently washed away the blood in his hair, she murmured softly. Abdullah did not know what she was saying. He could not concentrate on anything.

"It's a long gash," he heard her say as she cleaned his wound. "More than three inches long." Then he knew nothing more as darkness swept him into oblivion.

Zumrat caught his slumping body and guided him to the bed. She lifted his legs and tried to position him comfortably.

Before she called for help and took him to the hospital for stitches, she spent time in prayer for her husband. Why she was so sure this was a punishment from God, Zumrat did not know. But a deep feeling took hold of her, and she felt confident that somehow, in His own way, God was speaking to her husband.

Abdullah was bedfast for over a week as he recovered from his injury. Zumrat did everything she could to make him comfortable and never again mentioned the accident being a punishment from God. But Abdullah remembered. He had much time to think about what had happened and how his wife had reacted so strangely. He also had time to remember tearing up the New Testament. It was hard for him to think. His head ached frequently, and he felt disoriented. He wished he could think clearly.

After the accident, frequent headaches assailed him. Even after Abdullah recovered from his wound and returned to building the restaurant, the headaches never went away. Sometimes they were more bearable, but always his aching head bothered him.

There was something else too. He could not really put his finger on what his other problem was, but he found himself getting angry very easily. As months and then years passed, he would at times find himself extremely upset. There seemed to be no reason for his outbursts, and Abdullah always excused himself because of the blow to his head.

He was mentally affected as well. He had deep moody spells, and unrest drove his mind wild. Life was pressing on him from all sides, and a great darkness threatened to shut him away from everyone.

Chapter 8

"My head aches continually, and I have a hard time concentrating on anything," Abdullah told his mother.

"Where did you leave the children?" Miryam asked.

"I left all three with Zumrat's mother," Abdullah told her. "They are used to being with their grandmother while we both work."

Zumrat had been working as a telephone operator. She had quit her job for a while after their third child, another daughter, Dildora, had been born in 1986. Now she was working again.

"Son, you are not well. It has been more than four years since that blow to your head. Something is seriously wrong with you!"

It was true. Abdullah was having a hard time at work trying to cope with his frequent headaches and, even worse, his mental turmoil.

"It has affected our home too," he admitted. "Zumrat is trying hard to not get discouraged, but since my injury, she has to work. Though she doesn't complain, I know she is feeling the stress. That's why I insisted she go on this vacation."

It had not been easy for him to convince his wife to

leave. Zumrat had mentioned one evening in a laughing tone that her director had told the employees that they were all entitled to a ten-day vacation in India. Their expenses would be paid, and other people would cover for them while they were gone.

"The other women started making plans right away," she had told her husband. "But I told the director he won't have to find someone to replace me, for I can't go."

Abdullah had decided that his wife should go. At last she had consented, and now she was gone. He had taken the children to her mom's house the first day and tried to work. But today he had traveled across the city to visit his mother.

"I feel as though I am dying," he told his mother. "Slowly dying inside."

"Don't say that!" Miryam wailed. "It's bad luck to talk about dying! Allah will punish you!"

"Do you still believe in God?"

"Yes, son, I do. I think you should stop taking those pills your doctor is feeding you. You look all droopy, and your eyes are dull and lifeless. I have noticed it ever since you saw that doctor."

"I don't know. I can't think." Abdullah felt tired and old.

"That's just it. Come, I will pray for you!"

Abdullah's mother read a prayer from a book. The prayer petitioned some saints to plead with Allah for healing for the sick.

It didn't make sense. How could any saint, probably dead anyway, do anything for him? Could they go to God in the spirit world and ask for healing because they had been so good in their own lives? Abdullah knew enough about the priests who officiated in the mosques to know they did not live holy lives—at least not the ones he knew. They became drunk and used their position to try to better themselves. The saints were probably people like that. Plus, they could not know about his problem.

But, strangely, he felt better afterward. For the rest of the day, he felt relieved in his mind. It was a good feeling.

But it did not last. The next day the headaches came back, and his thoughts drove him into darkness again.

"I feel all empty inside," he told Alexander. "I can't describe it."

Wrinkling his forehead in concern, Alexander looked at his friend. Earlier he had encouraged Abdullah to go see a heart specialist. When the tests had come back showing his heart was sound and beating strong, he had encouraged him to go to a psychiatrist, who had given him the pills that made him feel dopey and all washed out. Plus, his headaches had not gone away.

"Tell you what," Alexander said decisively. "Those friends of Maria's who meet upstairs—we will go and ask them to pray for you. Maria tells me of people who have been healed from their sicknesses. Maybe they can help you."

"No," Abdullah said, shaking his head.

"It's something else to try. You're not getting better with all the help from the doctors. It's no big deal to go. They are friendly, and I'm sure Heinrich would pray for you. He's a good man. We can go right now. I know where he lives."

"I'm not interested. My mom prayed for me, and I felt better for a while, but it all came back again. Besides, Zumrat is still gone, and I don't want to stay away from home too long."

"Come with me." Alexander took him by the arm and began pulling him toward the house.

"It's something Christian, isn't it?"

"I won't tell anyone! You're not working at a state job anyway. No one needs to find out." Alexander did not give up. "For the sake of your health, let's try!"

But Abdullah refused. He loosened his friend's grip on his arm and went home.

"I went and asked Heinrich to pray for you," Alexander told him the next day. "I told him you were sick and needed help. He was very glad to pray for you. It was like he knew about your problems. Maria told me she has been praying for you."

Abdullah did not answer. How could their prayers help? Was there even a god who was concerned about people and their problems? He felt confused.

"Tell you what," Alexander continued. "Tonight after work, you come home with me. This is the evening they gather at our house for prayer. I will take you upstairs to the room where they meet and they can pray for you. It can't hurt!"

Perhaps because he was feeling desperate, Abdullah followed Alexander up the steps that evening. "We will just sit down and see what they say," Alexander had told him. "You don't have to do anything."

Abdullah breathed heavily, but it was not from climbing the stairs. He felt suffocated and tried to take deep breaths. His heart was pounding.

No one paid much attention when they entered the room. Abdullah sat down on a wooden chair beside Alexander and looked curiously at the small group of people sitting in a circle discussing something they had been studying.

"It is the Spirit inside of us who makes us free," a man, obviously the teacher, was saying. "We can not be truly free unless we have the Spirit of Jesus Christ."

Freedom! That was what he wanted! To be free from the thoughts that haunted him day and night—free from the darkness that wanted to swallow him!

A woman's voice broke in on his thoughts. It was Maria's. "I love how it says we have no condemnation if we believe in Jesus. I can sleep, go about my work, and live in perfect confidence, knowing I am not condemned anymore." Even though Alexander was shifting uneasily beside him, Abdullah was becoming absorbed in the conversation. Something about the discussion spoke directly to his heart. He hardly noticed when his friend quietly got up and left the room.

The more the group talked, the more questions Abdullah had. Did they really live the way they talked, putting other people before their own interests?

He looked at Maria. She did. And Zumrat. That was more and more the way his wife was living.

Almost to his surprise, when the man, whom Abdullah assumed must be Heinrich, asked for prayer requests, he stood up. "I would like for you to pray for me. For my health. I have a pain in my head, and even though the doctor says I am fine, I feel a constant pain in my heart," he said simply, then sat down again.

Heinrich nodded pleasantly and said, "We will pray."

As they knelt on the floor, Abdullah hesitated, then slid to his knees.

"Dear Lord, we pray for the needs in this home. We pray for Zumrat and for the children you have given this family. May you strengthen our sister with your love and support during this difficult time. We pray for Abdullah, that he can find you as the true answer for his spiritual needs." As Heinrich continued to pray, Abdullah listened keenly. How did he know about Zumrat and the children? Maybe Alexander had told him. Why was he not praying for his health? For his headache and for the pain in his heart? It was bewildering.

Prayers for other needs followed. Everyone prayed except Abdullah. After prayer one lady stood up.

"While we were praying for Zumrat, I saw a vision of a blue lake with pure water. A snow-white swan came swimming along, feeding along the bank. Another swan was swimming in the distance, and it seemed like it wanted to come close to the first swan. At times it came closer, then it would swim away."

Abdullah listened intently to the woman's soft voice. "While we were praying for Zumrat," the lady had said. Was the first swan his wife?

"Then," the woman continued, "the second swan finally swam up to the first swan, and when it did, they became whiter and brighter. They swam together for a while, feeding in the pure water, then they beat their snowy wings and flew away into the blue sky, headed for heaven."

Silence followed this revelation. Finally Heinrich spoke. "Zumrat has been coming to meet with us for four years, feeding spiritually on the words of the Bible. They have nourished her and fed her spiritual life. Now her husband Abdullah has come. He, too, will eat of this spiritual food. They will together be washed clean and white by the forgiveness of their sins and will minister together in the kingdom of God."

Abdullah was amazed. What in the world was this man saying? How could he know what would happen? Much more, why did he say that Zumrat had been coming here for four years?

He turned to the lady beside him. "What is he saying? I don't understand! Zumrat has been meeting with you for four years?"

She smiled. "Yes. She is one of us. Now it's your turn."

Anger swept over Abdullah. "I came here because Alexander said you would pray for my pain!" He looked around the room for his friend. "He left me here, and not once did anyone pray for my pain! Now you tell me my wife has been meeting with you! I did not know this!"

"We pray more for you to know Jesus than for you to get rid of your pain," the woman continued earnestly. "Often we have prayed with Zumrat for you, that you may learn to know who Jesus is!"

But Abdullah was no longer listening.

That night, Abdullah thrashed around in his bed. His anger had not left him. *How could she?* He thought. *What has been happening to me is all Zumrat's fault!* He thumped the pillow.

He ground his teeth in anguish. His wife was far away, on the vacation he had insisted she take, and now when he needed to ask her questions, to ask her why she had done this to him, she was gone!

She had left their religion and become a Christian! The religion from the West! No wonder he had such dark feelings and mental stress! She had brought it on him by forsaking their ways!

What were their ways, anyway? They were supposed to be Muslims, but even Abdullah knew they were not religious Muslims. Yet there was a feeling of betrayal somehow. Something uncanny had happened to them. It must be Zumrat's fault for having accepted Christianity.

What did he know about Christians? Very little, except that they believed in Jesus Christ as their Messiah, and that His Spirit could live inside of people. How was that possible when He had lived and died thousands of years ago?

But the people who called themselves Christians, like Maria and the others who were there that evening, did not fit his mental image of Christians. They did not wage wars against the Muslims like he had learned in the history books in school. He could not imagine Maria and Heinrich and his wife and the others marching in any crusades, killing innocent people and fighting against other religions. None of this made sense.

Praying for him! That was what they had been doing? Praying that he—what was it that woman had said?—would learn to know who Jesus is! No wonder his pain did not go away, no matter how many doctors he saw. No wonder his heart was so heavy. Those people had been praying for him!

He was angry with Alexander. He had taken him there and then left. Alexander was not a Christian, he was sure of that. The nerve to take him there while not even believing in their religion himself! Wait until he saw him again!

But most of all, he was angry with Zumrat. All this time she had not told him that she attended these meetings. True, she was often gone, but he assumed she was visiting her relatives and friends.

His thoughts became wilder and turned to revenge. He would get even with Zumrat for bringing all this trouble on their home. He would not allow her to leave the house, except to go to work. Every evening he would ask where she had been after work. He would force her to give up her religion.

His head pounded, but he ignored the pain. A war raged in his mind—a storm far fiercer than any he had experienced before.

Abdullah did not go to work the next day. Nor the next. He left the children with Zumrat's mother, and she did not ask why. He was so deeply tormented that he could not work. He could barely function. He stayed inside his house and did not talk to anyone. Alexander tried to talk to him, but Abdullah screamed at him and shut the door in his face.

Not one of his relatives could make any sense out of his behavior. They had never seen Abdullah so angry before. They shook their heads, bemoaning that Zumrat was gone and no one knew how to contact her.

She did not return the day she was expected, and they learned that she had decided to stay an extra four days.

This complication added fuel to Abdullah's rage. He wanted to talk to his wife. He had plenty of questions for her. He would ask the questions first, then he would have to kill her. That would get rid of the problems that were driving him wild. No longer would he have to bear the curse from having a Christian in his house!

In his saner moments, he thought about the children. Who

would take care of their children if their mother were dead? He knew he could not do it by himself, and Zumrat's parents would not take them forever.

Okay. He would not kill her—just force her to give up her faith, say she was sorry, and then he would control her. That way, if something happened to him, the children would at least have a mother.

At times Abdullah felt sure he was dying. He would lie on the bed and fold his hands over his chest, waiting for death. But as he waited, dark thoughts would creep over him and he would wonder what was going to happen to him after he died. He could not think away the darkness by telling himself that his body would just decay like other dead bodies and that would be the end of it. Something deep inside told him there was something more. Something after death for which he was not ready. He did not know what was going to happen, but he knew darkness was waiting for him. He was sure of that.

One night he found himself praying. He tried to pray to the god he remembered from his grandfather's stories. He wished he could talk to his grandfather. Where was he now that he had died? Where was his grandfather's god?

Whenever his thoughts drifted to the things he had heard that evening in Alexander's home, he pushed them away. He did not want to think of Jesus. He did not want to remember how they had talked about being free from condemnation. Jesus was just a man who had lived a long time ago and who now was dead. Yes, that was surely the way it was.

"God, do you exist? I want to know. I must know! If you exist, let me know. Why don't we know anything about you? Why are you so silent? Why don't you care about us? People say you exist, but no one can prove it. I don't even know why I'm talking to you. I don't know if you hear!" A feeling of despair swept over the anguished man and tears wet his pillow.

Something prodded him to get up and kneel beside the bed. He did not know why, but he was so desperate, so helpless, that he was willing to try anything to get answers.

"I am afraid to die! I don't want to die! If you exist, show yourself to me!"

No immediate answer swept down out of heaven. All was quiet. And dark. Nothing was different.

Abdullah crawled back into bed. Numbness seized his mind. He did not know what to do.

Zumrat would be coming home soon. It was her fault all this was happening to him. She would have to suffer.

As though another mind possessed him, he could not turn his thoughts from wanting to hurt his wife. He gritted his teeth. Just wait until she got back! Then see who was going to suffer!

Chapter 9

"I have never seen so many poor people before in my life!" Zumrat told Abdullah. "First in Pakistan, then in India! They were sitting along the streets, and little children no older than Daniel were begging for food! Our guide told us not to give them anything, for it would cause a stampede as they all rushed in to beg. I tell you, it was hard to refuse their big, round eyes." She rocked four-year-old Dildora in her arms and planted a kiss on the sleeping child. "Oh, it is so good to be home!"

Seven-year-old Daniel regarded his mother with big eyes. "Didn't they have a mama?" he asked.

"I don't know. It was chilly there, and I saw children trying to stay warm with some old blankets that were more holes than blanket. Poverty was everywhere."

Dilnoza stroked her mama's cheeks. "I am glad I have a mama."

Zumrat's arms encircled her oldest daughter lovingly. "I really missed you. It was interesting, but I was so ready to come home to my children. To my family," she added, looking into her husband's face.

Abdullah sat on a chair in the corner of the living

room. He had not entered the conversation, nor did he have any questions. Zumrat looked quizzically at her husband. He was even more silent than usual. And she had never before noticed that peculiar look in his eyes. Had it been there when she had left? She wasn't sure.

"I brought a shirt home for you," Zumrat spoke up, trying to get her husband to talk. Why did he just sit there, staring at her, then at the floor? He must still be suffering from the mental problems that had plagued him for the last several years. Fear clutched at her heart as she realized he was getting worse.

"Maybe I shouldn't have left. You needed me at home," she said in a soft tone. "I wish I . . ."

With a wave of his hand, Abdullah silenced her. He got up and left the room. The eyes of his family followed him.

"Well, now I am home! Let's get ready for bed, and tomorrow you will see some of the things I brought back from my trip." Zumrat forced her voice to stay calm and even. Inside, she was trying to still her racing heart. Where had Abdullah gone?

The children kissed their mother and hurried upstairs to bed. The hallway was not heated, and their rooms were not as warm as downstairs. The two girls shared a room, and Daniel had his own.

It was over an hour later and Zumrat was in bed when Abdullah finally returned. She heard him pacing back and forth in the living room. He was more agitated tonight than she ever remembered him being before. She heard the back door slam as he left the house again.

Abdullah had been very quiet when he had picked her up at the airport. He had hardly said more than hello, then he had grabbed her luggage and carried it to their car. All the way home she had tried to talk to him, but he had just hunched his shoulders and responded with as few words as possible.

Zumrat turned the pillow under her head. It felt lumpy, and she tried to smooth it. Her thoughts turned to prayers as once more she prayed for her husband, for herself, and for their children. "Lord, I don't know what is going to happen to us! Please help me not to be scared. You know the situation is getting worse. Abdullah's mind is very disturbed. I will trust in you. I believe in your promise that you will never leave me nor forsake me. Help me say and do the right thing."

She sat up in bed and snapped on the bedside lamp. She would try to talk to her husband. Getting up, she put on her coat and slipped on her shoes. She went outside and saw Abdullah in the backyard, staring off into the darkness. She closed the back door, and he turned to look at her.

As Zumrat walked toward him, she said, "Please! There seems to be something on your mind. What is wrong? You don't talk to me or ask anything about my trip. What is wrong, Abdullah?" Anxiety made her voice sharper than she wanted it to be.

"What do you want from me?" The words leaped out of his mouth.

"I—I just want us to talk. You seem so distant."

Abdullah began breathing heavily. "So you think this is a simple matter? You betrayed our god! You accepted a new faith! A Christian faith!" He began trembling all over, and hot, bitter tears pooled in his eyes.

Zumrat took a deep breath, startled by the vehemence in his voice.

"You prayed for me! Because you did this, I am damned! My life is ruined! Our lives are ruined! My children now have a mother who has forsaken our Muslim ways. Our plans are doomed! Our children will have to suffer all their lives because of you!" He spoke loudly and quickly.

"Wait! Let me explain!" Zumrat said. "You do not understand how it works! Come, come inside. The neighbors will hear us arguing."

Abdullah faced his wife in the kitchen. "Why have you done this? Don't you know what happens when we forsake our heritage? We will forever be marked, and our children will not be accepted into society. It is entirely your fault! You have been meeting in secret for the last four years. You betrayed me! I cannot let this go on!" He trembled as he spoke and grabbed the edge of the kitchen counter. "You are guilty!" he screamed at her.

Zumrat backed away from him. Never had she seen him so angry. "But—but we are not practicing Muslims! We do not go to prayers or attend the mosque! I thought you did not believe in Allah!"

"That doesn't matter! We are Muslims!" He banged his fist on the countertop. "You have been meeting with these Christians and asking them to pray for me, haven't you?"

"What happened?" Zumrat asked, trying to make sense of her husband's conversation. "What do you know?"

Speaking through clenched teeth, Abdullah explained slowly, "I went to one of their meetings because Alexander said they could pray for my headaches. There I found out that they knew all about us! About me!" he yelled. "They know about me! They didn't even pray for my headaches! They prayed for you and the children! They said I should get to know Jesus!"

Zumrat could not believe her ears. Abdullah had attended a prayer meeting? With Alexander? Whatever had made him do such a thing?

"Now I suffer. Because of your prayers! Because of the prayers of Heinrich and those people!" He almost spat out the words. "You are the reason I have this pain in my head that won't go away! You are the reason I can't sleep and why I can't work and why I have such deep problems! It's all because of you!

"You wanted me to speak! Well, now I'm speaking!" He waved his finger under her nose. "If it were not for you, I would be well. We would be rich by now, and we would all have a future. You have ruined it all!"

Zumrat began crying.

"Now you cry! I tell you, you must leave this foreign belief! You must leave these Christians and their Jesus! I will not have it!"

Turning in agitation, he looked blankly at the kitchen cabinets. Then he turned on her again.

"Why are you standing there crying? Why are you silent? You always have words. Where are they now?" he taunted.

"I'm sorry," Zumrat said through her tears. "I should have told you I was meeting with the Christians. I should have told you that I repented and now believe in Jesus. I wanted to show you by my life that I am a different woman so you, too, would believe in Him. Now I see that I should not have kept this from you."

Taking a step closer to his wife, Abdullah said, "All this time you have been praying for me I have suffered. Now I will make you suffer. You will suffer!" Then, his voice low and sinister, he said, "I will kill you for what you have done to me!"

The words hung in the silence that followed. Zumrat looked squarely into her husband's enraged eyes. She could see he was dead serious.

She licked her dry lips. Her first instinct was to try to run . . . run anywhere—away from her demented husband. But what about the children? What would he do to them?

"Please!" She held up her hand as if to stop him. "Don't do this!"

Abdullah was breathing heavily. He stepped closer to her, clenching his powerful hands.

Then, as quickly as thought and as softly as a protecting shield, quietness came over Zumrat. Looking up calmly, she said, "Give me five minutes to pray."

Without waiting for a reply, she slipped to her knees and began weeping. "O Lord, I am sorry I hid my actions from my husband. I did not tell him I was going to meet with the other Christians. Forgive me and make my heart clean before you. I want to come to you with all my sins forgiven.

"I know you love me. I love you, Lord Jesus! Prepare me for whatever is going to happen. I place all my trust in you." Then, crying and praying in a loud voice, she said, "O Lord, do not punish me for what I have done!

"Be with the children when I am gone. O God, forgive Abdullah for what he is doing. He does not understand your love. I pray that someday he will find you so he can find happiness. I say goodbye to my family. I give them into your hands."

With her face lifted toward heaven, Zumrat did not even close her eyes. She was looking upward, and a heavenly peace filled her heart. "Oh, thank you! You are here, right with me! I can feel it!" She lifted her hands toward the ceiling.

Abdullah's face loomed over her. His eyes, enormous through her tears, seemed to be staring right into her heart.

The kingdom of darkness was trying to dominate her. She could feel an evil power swirling around her, and as she saw her husband's face coming closer and closer, she saw images of demons all around his eyes.

"Lord Jesus! Save me!" Her desperate cry went winging upward to her Saviour. "I give myself into your hands!" She closed her eyes to hide the hideous scene. Then she bowed her head and waited.

As she quieted, she felt herself being lifted off the kitchen floor. Gently, easily, she was being transported upward as though in a soft cloud. She could almost feel the loving arms of Jesus holding her close. Then a strange sound penetrated her vision—the sound of a man weeping.

When Zumrat opened her eyes, her mouth fell open in wonder. Abdullah was kneeling beside her, and, in an entirely different voice, he was speaking. No, he was praying! In awe, she listened.

"God, do you really hear people when they talk to you like Zumrat talked to you? Can you help us? If you are real, help me. I want to change. I want something different. I want to be happy!" Bitter tears coursed down his cheeks and his shoulders shook. He put his hands over his face and continued to cry, "Please, God, help me! Help me! I can't live this way!"

A flood of compassion swept over Zumrat as she sensed her husband's agony. Placing her hand gently on his shoulder, she wept with him.

"God, help me! Oh, God, help me!" Over and over he prayed those heart-wrenching words.

"Abdullah! Pray to God in the name of Jesus! He only hears when we pray in Jesus' name. Then your cries for help will be heard!" The Holy Spirit moved in Zumrat to speak to her husband. "Pray in the name of Jesus!"

His body jerked violently. He stiffened. He turned to look at Zumrat. "What's the difference?"

"Here is the test," Zumrat told him, looking directly at him. "If Jesus is God, let him show his power to you. If Jesus is not God, nothing will happen."

Slowly, as though he was exploring something completely foreign to his thinking, he began speaking again. "Jesus, if you are real, I will not harm my wife. If you are not real, I must do what I intended to do."

Zumrat listened. She waited in faith for whatever was going to happen. Her life was hanging in the balance.

"If the words my wife is saying are true, then Jesus, you are God. I want to know! I have to know! If you are real, I will tell other people. I will tell everyone that you are God!"

Praying with all her heart, Zumrat's voice rose and fell in her desire to see her husband's prayers answered. "Lord Jesus, reveal yourself to him! Save his soul!"

All the frustrations of Abdullah's life had come to one pivotal point. Nothing he had ever lived for sustained him now. He saw his life as empty and meaningless. He felt he had nothing inside of him. He was completely empty and hollow.

Talking to God in the name of Jesus was not easy. Yet Zumrat had told him that was the only way God would hear him. How was it possible that Jesus could be God? He must know! "Oh, Jesus, help! If you are God, show it! Let me know somehow!"

Then a strange thing happened. The kitchen ceiling above him began moving like a large piece of paper. The walls disappeared, and the white began to slowly change into a lovely shade of blue, as the sky on a beautiful, clear day. From out of the blue, a warm glow shimmered and became brighter. Then more lights appeared, and one light became brighter and brighter. As it moved toward him, Abdullah gazed in open wonder. The form of a man dressed in white became visible in the light. The man moved, and Abdullah saw his hands and feet. Lifting his head, he looked at the man's face.

What he saw filled him with wonder. The eyes were so loving, so kind and gentle, and they looked straight into Abdullah's heart. The lips were smiling. Smiling at him!

Glancing down at where he was kneeling, Abdullah saw in horror that he was all dirty and everything around him was gray. In the presence of the shining purity of the man in front of him, he felt terrible.

With a desperate struggle, Abdullah tried to flee from the dirt. He began saying, "Lord Jesus, forgive me! Forgive me for having doubted you! Forgive the sins of my youth! Forgive me for not having believed in you!" On and on he prayed, asking forgiveness for everything that came to his mind. "I am sorry I have been so bad to Zumrat. I am sorry I have not been a good daddy to my children." The words tumbled out of his mouth.

Then something even more wonderful happened. The figure of the man, whom he now knew was Jesus, came closer and began stepping down a golden ladder toward him. Holding out his hands, the figure stopped, and a flame of fire descended on top of Abdullah's head, right on the scar. A peculiar sensation filled him from his head to his feet. He felt the healing power fill his entire body. Suddenly he was laughing and crying and praising God. "Now I know you are God! Thank you, Jesus! I know you are God!"

When he woke from his trance, he was lying on the kitchen floor, drenched in sweat and breathing heavily. Zumrat was kneeling beside him, mopping his face with a towel. "O Jesus, heal my husband! Give him peace in his heart!"

So Zumrat had not seen the vision! She did not know he had seen Jesus!

Rising from the floor, Abdullah went to his wife. Reaching for her, he said in a broken voice, "Oh, my dear wife, I am so sorry! I was wrong for what I was going to do to you! Jesus is God! He is! He really is God!" Hugging her to him, he cried brokenly on her shoulder. "I am so sorry! Please forgive me!"

Still clinging to one another, they prayed together. Their tears mingled as they talked and prayed. At times they hardly knew to whom they were talking as they opened their hearts to each other and to God.

"My children! Oh, I must see them!" Abdullah suddenly drew away from Zumrat and ran upstairs.

"My son!" Abdullah whispered and bent over, kissing the sleeping boy's cheek. "Oh, my son!" He could say no other words as he silently wept. Zumrat followed him upstairs and encircled his waist with her arm.

Then they went to the little girls' room, and Abdullah kissed their innocent faces as they slept.

"I will call Heinrich! I will share the good news with him!" Zumrat said as they returned downstairs. Abdullah was still walking around, lifting his hands in wonder and thanking God.

"Zina, this is Zumrat. Listen, I have wonderful news! Abdullah believes in Jesus! He is a Christian! Tell Heinrich! We want you to know this! A wonderful thing has happened to us!"

Abdullah stepped up to Zumrat's side. As she listened for a reply, he noticed her frown. "Zina, do you hear me? Abdullah is a Christian."

With a smile, Zumrat hung up. She turned to her husband and laughed, "I don't know if she understood. She kept saying 'huh?' then finally she said, 'okay.' But I had to let them know."

Then, looking at the clock, she said, "Oh, no wonder! Look, it's four o'clock already! No wonder she sounded confused!"

Abdullah smiled at her. "I don't know if I can sleep, although I feel more at rest than I ever have in my life." Then he stopped and said, "My pain! The headache! It's gone! Completely gone!" He lifted his hand to his head and felt the scar. Yes, it was still there.

"Jesus healed me! Not only did he heal my heartache, he healed my body!" Awe filled him, and once more the two knelt and thanked God for answering the prayers of their hearts.

"Jesus, you are God! You really, really are God! Thank you! Thank you!" On into the morning, the newly born man offered up his thanks.

Chapter 10

"Good morning, children!" Abdullah could not keep the joy in his heart from spilling over. "Jesus is God!"

Zumrat sat at the other end of the breakfast table, her eyes shining with unshed tears of joy. The short night had left her body tired, but her spirit was overflowing with happiness. She had a new husband.

"Good morning, Papa," Daniel answered dutifully. Then he looked closely at his father. Was this smiling man his daddy?

The two girls also replied to their father's greeting. Why was Daddy smiling so much?

"Children, I want to tell you what a wonderful thing happened last night. I saw Jesus in a vision, and now I know He is God. Jesus has taken away all my sins and burdens, and now I am clean and free. My headache is gone, and even better, my heartache is gone. You have a new daddy!"

The three children's dark eyes stared in amazement as Abdullah spoke. They had hardly ever heard their father speak more than one sentence at a time. Now he was speaking at length, and speaking with joy. They looked at their mother and knew everything was all right, because Mama was smiling—smiling at them and at Daddy.

"I am glad, Papa," Daniel managed to say. A smiling, happy daddy was something quite wonderful!

After breakfast, the telephone rang and Zumrat answered. "Hello, this is Zina. I had a really strange dream. I dreamed that you called in the night and said Abdullah was praying. I had to call you and tell you about it. Maybe God will soon answer our prayers."

Zumrat didn't know whether to laugh or to cry. "Zina," she choked out, "something wonderful has happened! Abdullah . . ." then she could not speak anymore. The long years of waiting, the hundreds of prayers for her husband, and all the strain she had been under were finally over. She sobbed into the phone.

"My dear Zumrat, what is it? Oh, Heinrich, come here. No . . . wait. We'll be right over."

In less than twenty minutes, the pastor and his wife were on their doorstep. Zumrat hurried to the door and said, "Oh, come in! God has done a wonderful work in our home!"

Abdullah was in the front hall, waiting for the couple. "I know that Jesus is alive! He is my Lord!"

Then Zina fell into Zumrat's waiting arms and Heinrich embraced the joyful Abdullah. "Praise be to Jesus Christ, our Lord. He is worthy of praise and glory and honor. Oh, brother, we rejoice with you. Tell us all about it."

There was nothing formal about that little meeting in Abdullah and Zumrat's living room. The three children listened in awe as their daddy told the excited visitors what had happened that night.

"Now I have no more pain." Abdullah reached up and touched the scar on his head. "For the first time in four years, I have no pain whatsoever. I am healed. In my head and in my heart. I have no more animosity toward life. Toward anyone. I feel like . . . like a new person."

Heinrich laughed. "You are a new person. The Bible says, 'Old things are passed away; behold, all things are become new.' Now you know why we use the term 'born again.'"

Nodding, Abdullah agreed. "I am born again. Oh, I need to tell my mother! I want to tell Alexander! I must tell everyone I know what has happened!"

"Let's pray together." Heinrich knelt on the floor. "Come, children, kneel down and pray with your parents. We will all pray."

Never before had the children seen their father kneel. They had seen their mother on her knees many times when Daddy was gone, but now they saw Daddy on his knees, praising Jesus in a loud voice.

Zumrat's heart was overflowing with emotions as she began praying and weeping with joy at the wonderful change in her husband's heart. Heinrich and Zina, lifting their hands toward heaven, joined them in prayer, filling the room with praise. As the angels in heaven rejoiced that another man had joined the kingdom of Jesus Christ, the three children listened in wonder.

"I must go tell my mother!" Abdullah repeated after Heinrich and his wife had reluctantly gone.

Abdullah would not be working today. After calling Alexander on the telephone and babbling almost incoherently to him, he did finally manage to let him know he was not coming to work. He let Zumrat talk to Maria and heard her tell her friend the wonderful story.

"Oh, I can't wait until you see him, Maria! His eyes are all shiny, and he just keeps smiling!" Zumrat's voice showed her joy.

After Daniel left for school, Abdullah and Zumrat took the little girls to see Abdullah's mother.

"*Babushka* (grandma)! Oh, mother! Where are you?" Abdullah called as soon as they entered his mother's house.

The empty house echoed his call. They heard no answering footsteps.

Abdullah walked through the hall and into the kitchen. He looked out the window and saw his mother in the backyard.

"Mother! Something wonderful has happened!" He burst out the back door, and when he saw his mother turning to greet him, he ran up to her and threw his arms around her and began weeping loudly.

"Abdullah!" the elderly woman burst out in surprise. "What happened to you?"

Too emotional to reply, Abdullah kissed his mother's cheeks again and again. "Oh, I am so sorry for every wicked thing I have ever done. Please forgive me for not having been a good son to you."

The old woman was overcome by the weeping man in her arms. Crying with her son, she looked up at Zumrat, standing in the doorway. "What is wrong with him? Oh, is he crazy? My son, my son!"

"No, he's not crazy, Mama." Zumrat's voice rang out in the yard.

"Come inside. It's too cold out here." Abdullah's mother didn't know what was going on, but she wanted to get inside her house. Maybe then she could make sense of everything.

"Calm down and tell me what happened," she said when she finally got Abdullah seated beside her on the couch. Looking at Zumrat, she asked, "Was he at the hospital? Did they get a new treatment for him?" She could tell by the look on her daughter-in-law's face that something good had happened.

"No, Mama," Abdullah finally managed to say. "I was not at the hospital. I have found God."

With a sharp breath, his mother asked, "What? How can you say you have found God?"

"Mama, Jesus is God. He is the God we have wanted all our

lives." And to his mother's astonished ears, he recounted once again his wonderful story.

"You are demented. You saw a man in white you call Jesus." Turning to Zumrat for help, she said, "You must take him to the doctor." Then, in agitation, she turned to face her son again. "Oh, I am thankful your father is not alive to see this! How can you say that Jesus is God? You have forsaken your religion! We are Muslims!"

Sadly Abdullah corrected his mother. "My heart aches that I did not know this sooner! I would give all I have to be able to share this good news with my father. Oh, that he had not died before I found the Lord Jesus!"

The old woman had many questions for her son that day. Abdullah often did not know the answer. If Zumrat knew, she explained it to them both.

Suddenly Abdullah stopped and stared at Zumrat. "The book I burned—it was the New Testament! How could I have done such a thing? Oh, God, forgive me!" He wept bitterly at the thought of his earlier deed.

"Do not despair," Zumrat said gently. "We now have several New Testaments, and I'm sure Heinrich will make it possible for you to have one."

"I must have one!" Abdullah cried out. "I must learn more about Jesus. I must learn all I can about Him."

"Alexander, let me tell you what has happened to me," Abdullah told his friend the next morning as the two went to work. "I can hardly keep from shouting!"

"I see," his friend told him, chuckling. "I hear."

"Jesus is Lord! He is the Saviour for the entire world! He answers prayers and heals us from our sins!" Abdullah could not stop speaking.

Alexander nodded and walked briskly.

"I am a new man!" Abdullah continued. "I am healed from my headache! My heart is healed!"

"I am glad for you," Alexander said. "Your headache sure was getting you down."

"Not as much as my heartache. I was going crazy." Then he remembered. "Oh, Alexander, thank you for forcing me to go with you to where Heinrich was conducting that prayer meeting. Now I know what they were doing. I understand."

Grinning self-consciously, Alexander said nothing.

"Do you understand what happened to me?" Abdullah asked again.

"Maria told me. She said you were healed."

"Maria," Abdullah remembered. "I can't wait to see her and thank her. It was through her that Zumrat first heard about Jesus, and through her that I first saw someone who loved Jesus. Oh, how good God is!"

Then, with a slight frown, he turned once more to his friend. "Alexander, do you believe in Jesus? Have you repented of your sins?"

With a little laugh, Alexander joked, "I let Maria take care of the spiritual things in our home. She is much better at it than I am."

His answer bothered Abdullah. He remembered how Alexander had left him in the room with the believers.

"Oh, friend, no one can believe for you. It is something you must do yourself. You have to cry out to Jesus to save you." Abdullah witnessed boldly to his friend.

"Yes, yes," Alexander smoothed it away. "I hear that from my wife as well."

A dart pierced Abdullah's heart as he heard those words, and he determined to faithfully pray for his good friend, as others had faithfully prayed for him the past four years.

Abdullah could not convince his mother to attend meetings with them. But faithfully, almost daily, he went to visit her, telling her about the wonderful things he was reading in the New Testament. He would read the Scriptures to her, and she in turn would quote from the Koran.

Abdullah's mother had always tried to religiously follow the teachings of Mohammed. She had prayed daily for herself and her family. Now her son was telling her that Jesus was God.

That Abdullah was a changed man, no one could deny— not her, not her relatives, not any of Abdullah's friends. They hardly knew him anymore. The moody, sulky man had changed overnight. Literally. Now he went about telling all who would listen what wonderful things God had done for him, all in the name of Jesus Christ.

That first year of his salvation, Abdullah read the New Testament seventeen times. Over and over again he marveled that, at each successive reading, he learned so many more new things. He responded to the precious words and grew in his faith in Jesus.

His mother saw all this. Perhaps it was the joy and peace in her son's life that first penetrated her heart. After accompanying her son to the meetings and hearing the Gospel story several times, one evening she responded to the altar call and went forward to pray. "I believe Jesus is the Son of God. He is God."

Abdullah could barely restrain himself. "Mother! Oh, how I praise God for this day! How marvelous you are, Lord Jesus!"

In the same spot where he and Zumrat had been baptized, Abdullah's mother sealed her faith by water baptism. Outside, under the blue summer sky, the elderly lady gladly waded out into the river and answered the pastor's question with, "I believe that Jesus Christ is Lord. He is my Lord." Then, while the waiting group of believers sang a hymn, she was baptized.

Wrapping his arms around his mother, Abdullah's tears fell

unashamedly onto her soaking, white clothes. His mother was a Christian! Words of praise and wonder filled his mouth, and he began to pray. How greatly he rejoiced to see this day!

Chapter 11

The cargo planes landed on the immense field with military precision, their roar filling Abdullah's ears. He wanted to run but felt trapped. In horror and fascination he watched the scene unfold before him.

As soon as the planes landed, huge doors opened from the belly of the aircraft and ramps slid down. Down the ramps and onto the fields came armored tanks. Then, from the side doors, men dressed in army fatigues rushed out, carrying automatic rifles.

"O Lord!" Abdullah prayed. "Save us! Save our country!"

As the vision faded, he remembered where he was—in church, praying with the believers for their country and for their safety. A murmur of voices filled Alexander and Maria's house. More than a hundred and fifty people now gathered regularly for services. The Word of God was spreading, and people were repenting and coming to know Jesus.

Heinrich and Zina, their faithful pastor and his wife, knelt beside him. Maria was nearby, faithful in her testimony of loving the Lord even though Alexander still had not made a profession of faith in Christ.

Abdullah's mother attended whenever she could, and in spite of the ridicule and taunts from her relatives and Muslim neighbors, she had a wonderful testimony and told people everywhere of the saving power of Jesus.

Zumrat's sister Sofia and her husband Aziz had been strong believers ever since their son Sherzat had been healed. Now they had another son, Begzod, only a year younger than his older brother, and he, too, remained healthy and strong. "We now have two healthy sons because of the power of Jesus Christ!" The parents were outspoken and told anyone who was interested about the miracle God had done in their family.

Many others had responded to the Gospel as well. As the believers humbled themselves before the Lord and faithfully testified of God's wonderful change in their lives, many repented and accepted Jesus as their Lord. The church grew, and believers met regularly in other parts of the city.

"I had a vision during prayer," Abdullah told the group after their Bible study that evening. He recounted the disturbing military planes descending onto the field and the tanks and armed men deplaning.

For a moment all was silent, then an elderly sister spoke up. "God is telling us that trouble is coming to our land. We must warn everyone to repent and turn to Jesus Christ, the Son of the living God."

"I, too, had a vision," another believer spoke up. "I saw a city, and there was blood flowing in the streets."

"These visions surely are signs to us from the Lord," Heinrich told the group. "God wants us to prepare our hearts to be strong and faithful. We are not guaranteed safety in troublesome times, but we are given a promise from Jesus Himself: 'I will never leave thee, nor forsake thee.' Let us examine our hearts and put away all sin from our lives." Then he read Amos 3:6-7.

" 'Shall a trumpet be blown in the city, and the people not be afraid? Shall there be evil in a city, and the Lord hath not done it? Surely the Lord God will do nothing, but he revealeth his secret unto his servants the prophets.'

"Only as we remain pure in our hearts before the Lord will we be able to properly discern the signs of the times," Heinrich concluded.

Once more the group prayed. The visions were foremost in their minds, and they asked that God would give them the strength to remain faithful no matter what lay ahead.

"Arvat, do you not feel a space deep inside you that longs for answers?" Abdullah asked, looking intently at his cousin.

"Why do you talk about such things all the time?" Arvat shifted on the bed. "Ever since we came for grandfather's funeral, you have talked about God and your strange belief that He had a Son. Why are the old ways not good enough for you?"

Abdullah sat on the edge of the bed he shared with his cousin. Shaking his head, he said simply, "Because Jesus has made such an enormous difference in my life. Cousin, I cannot help but talk about it! Jesus wants to do the same for everyone!"

"That I heard," Arvat replied. "When you talked to our cousin Oleg, he mocked you long and hard. I did admire how you stood up to him, for ever since he joined the KGB his superior attitude and boasting have been almost unbearable. But why do you constantly badger all of us with your beliefs? Why can't you leave us alone?"

"I want to tell you another reason. I want to tell you about a vision I had." Then Abdullah told his cousin about the military planes landing and about the blood in the city.

"How is this?" Arvat laughed. "We are living in a peaceful time. There is no war. The Uzbeks within our borders are, of course, discontent, but they always have been. They are not strong enough to cause any trouble. Your vision, as you call it, means nothing!"

"I do not want you to believe in Jesus because of the vision I had," Abdullah said sincerely. "God gave me this vision for a purpose, and I will tell people about it. But the greatest reason that I believe in Jesus is because of the healing he has done in my heart. You don't know the pain and suffering I had before! Arvat, I was going crazy!"

"Yes, I know. Our entire family knew something was wrong with you." He yawned and pulled the covers up to his chin. "I guess you're just a lucky man."

Lucky! Abdullah wanted to convince his cousin that it was much more than luck. It was the hand of God in his life! Yet he knew the Holy Spirit would have to grip his cousin's heart. Silently he prayed that Arvat would learn to know the wonderful cleansing power of faith in Jesus.

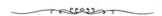

"Come in! Welcome!" Abdullah invited his cousin into their home.

"You are a prophet!" Arvat exclaimed after he had embraced Abdullah. "That vision you told me about four months ago—it happened! How did you know?"

Zumrat heard their voices and joined the men in the living room. She pulled the curtains against the night and went to make tea.

"When the uprising started, I could not believe it at first. But almost right away I remembered you telling me your vision after Grandfather's funeral. I knew then that what God let you see was real. It happened!" Arvat said earnestly.

"Yes, it did happen," Abdullah replied. "I am thankful that God allowed us to know about it beforehand. All during the fighting we kept praying for the people in our city. In those troubled times many more people repented and believed in Jesus. It was a bad time for the city, but God used it to speak to the hearts of those who were ready to listen to the Gospel."

"Such a war!" Arvat continued, shaking his head. "Those Uzbeks! Always fighting for more land. Even though they outnumber us here in Osh, we are still under the protection of the Kyrgyz government. They were soundly beaten back. I guess they will remember that lesson."

"Jesus said there will always be wars," Abdullah told him. "As long as people do not have peace in their hearts, the passions of men will continue to flare up and cause all kinds of problems on this earth. That is why we preach the good news of Jesus Christ. Even many who are not at war in their countries have their own private wars."

Zumrat brought in tea and offered a cup to their visitor.

"Thank you," Arvat said, looking into the cup thoughtfully. "I guess since you are a prophet, I do not need to hide my own troubles from you."

"I would much rather be called a servant of Jesus Christ," Abdullah chuckled. "I do not claim any supernatural ability to look into the future."

"I have a problem with my wife. Yeveka is ruining my life with her strong spirit. As our children get older, she is turning them against me. Just yesterday our oldest daughter, who as you know is not even twelve yet, flatly defied me, and Yeveka took her side and told her my demands were ridiculous. Now, what man can take that?"

On into the night, Abdullah shared with his cousin how Jesus Christ came to bring peace. He and Zumrat shared the struggles they had had earlier in their marriage.

"Jesus changed my heart when I prayed to him," Abdullah said sincerely. "Instead of blaming Zumrat for bringing trouble into my life, I now saw that God had given me a good wife. I learned to talk to her about my struggles and feelings. Before, I did not know how to share my deep feelings. God put a love in my heart for my family that I did not know existed. He set me free!"

Zumrat nodded. "I used to resent that Abdullah would not take responsibility when the children did something wrong. I always thought he was weak and did not care. When I became a believer, I realized that my strong will kept my husband from doing his duty. Before he could even correct the children, I was already on their case. Then, when things did not turn out well, I blamed him.

"I remember one of my good friends once told me, 'Try letting your husband take care of the problem. Say nothing for at least five minutes.' I thought that was ridiculous! I was sure that if I did not step in and take care of the situation, chaos would follow. Yet the Spirit pressed on me to wait. I had to bite my tongue to keep from speaking, but it worked! Abdullah now felt free to be the leader, and he corrected the children in a much more loving way." Zumrat paused, then laughed. "I have learned much about patience from my dear husband!"

Abdullah flushed slightly under his wife's praise. Turning to his cousin, he said, "Arvat, let Jesus change your life. We are not special people, except that we are changed by the power of Jesus Christ. He can change your heart! He can make your marriage work!"

"I know I need something," Arvat admitted. "When all that fighting erupted, I was scared. Somehow I knew I was not ready to die. I have done too much wrong in my life. I'm all black inside."

With tears in his eyes, Abdullah knelt beside his cousin. "Come, let us pray and tell the Lord Jesus all about it. Jesus really cares for you, Arvat!"

The hours stretched on into the night as they prayed and talked.

Great was the joy as another soul was added to the kingdom. As in the days of the Acts of the Apostles, many came to the kingdom of God, adding to the number of believers in Osh.

"If you don't stop preaching, there will be trouble." The short man accosted Abdullah as he walked up the path to his home. "We do not want any disturbance in our neighborhood."

Abdullah looked at the man who brought the warning. He hardly knew Ari, although they were next-door neighbors. But he did know that Ari had recently become a more zealous Muslim, for when the call for prayer sounded out over the city, he had seen his neighbor kneel.

"I speak what God wants me to say," Abdullah said without bitterness. "If I have something good to tell people, how can I stop? I must obey God rather than man."

"We know what you are doing!" hissed the agitated man. "All over the city people are turning away from our traditions, away from the teachings of the Koran, because of the Western religion you teach. You will suffer for this!"

Now was not the time to argue, but Abdullah could not help saying, "I teach no Western religion. I teach the truth. Jesus Christ is the truth!"

This time, Ari did not speak. He shouted. "You are damned! We know what is going on! We know you travel about the city, preaching to the people! Don't say I didn't warn you! The priests themselves sent me, and I want you to know they are watching. They know all about you. They know the names of the people who are attending your meetings. You will be stopped!"

"Excuse me," Abdullah said, and, walking around the agitated man, he went into his house.

"They are watching us," he told the group of believers that evening as they gathered for prayer. He did not have to explain who "they" were. All knew.

As the believers had increased and the work of the church had become known in Osh, the Muslim priests had not been idle. Indeed, just the opposite.

An upheaval on government levels had opened a chasm, and into that void the Muslim extremists had begun to push their own agenda. They spread teachings of *jihad,* or holy war, and many formerly moderate Muslims became fanatical followers of the charismatic leaders. The movement picked up momentum, especially among the young people. More and more people were adopting the strict Muslim dress, and now the women wore *burkas* and the men dressed in the tunics and hats of their religious party.

"Yes, more than once I've noticed a stranger in our Sunday worship services," Heinrich agreed. "They are gathering information."

"I was asked just last week what my address is," a middle-aged man told the group. "I noticed a long list of names on his paper."

"We need to be careful," Abdullah said. "We're definitely being watched."

"I will continue to speak about the saving power of Jesus Christ," a young believer said. "Didn't the early Christians face the same thing? We need to be willing to die for our faith."

A murmur of agreement rippled through the group.

"I am not afraid of what man can do to us," Abdullah continued soberly. "Yet we must continue to prepare ourselves. When persecution comes, we want to be strong in our faith. We want to be able to endure hardships as good soldiers of Christ."

As they discussed the impending trouble, they once more knelt and prayed.

Truly, the church had grown rapidly. In the summer of 1992, more than fifty new believers were baptized in the Akbura River.

The cold mountain waters did not deter those who had repented from their sins and were willing to make a public declaration of their faith in the Lord Jesus Christ.

This time Abdullah helped with the baptisms, for he had been ordained by the church as a pastor. The church greatly appreciated his love for Jesus and his simple, direct teachings. The three-hour-long baptismal service was filled with solid biblical teaching, and songs of praise and worship went winging upward into the blue, blue sky. Great was the rejoicing among the believers as they saw the number of people responding to the Gospel.

But even as gray clouds appeared on the horizon that afternoon, Abdullah noticed several strangers taking in the scene on the riverbanks. He felt the Spirit telling him that conflict was coming. The believers would be tested.

"Prepare us, O Lord," he prayed earnestly. "Make us strong in you. Do not let fear rule our lives!"

Chapter 12

"Dilnoza, where is your little sister?" Zumrat asked, setting down the empty teacup.

"Mama, she is over there," seven-year-old Dildora replied, pointing to the corner of the meeting hall.

"Have you heard from Abdullah yet?" Maria asked.

Just then the door to the street opened and two men walked into the room. They glanced quickly around the room, then walked up to where the two ladies were finishing their tea.

"We are looking for Abdullah Jousoupjanov," the taller of the two men said, smiling in a peculiar manner.

"He is not here," Zumrat said, rising to her feet and pulling her daughters to her side.

Once more the two men scanned the room. A crowd of around thirty people were still milling about after the Sunday morning service, many of them drinking their usual tea.

"Where is he?" the speaker asked, this time forgetting to smile.

"What we want," the shorter, older man interrupted, "is to know more about Jesus. Can you tell us about him?"

The two women glanced at each other. Then Maria spoke up. "We will let you talk with Abdullah's brother, Abdulatip. We need to take our children home." She looked around and saw her son Arnold talking with Daniel.

When Abdulatip saw Maria beckon to him, he walked over. "Yes?" he asked politely.

"Is there someplace we can talk privately?" the taller man asked. "Are you sure Abdullah Jousoupjanov is not here? He is your leader, is he not?"

"Abdullah is not here," Abdulatip answered patiently. "Why do you wish to see him?"

"Oh, that's all right," the short man said quickly as another man from the fellowship strode toward them. "Can you tell us about Jesus?"

Olubek joined the small circle, and he and Abdulatip began to talk quietly with the strangers.

"Boys, come," Zumrat called, and she and Maria left with their children.

"That was a strange request," Zumrat commented once they were outside.

Maria nodded, "I think they were more interested in finding Abdullah than they were in hearing about anything spiritual."

"Why do you think they wanted Abdullah?"

Looking at her friend, Maria said, "It is good that your husband is in Sweden. Remember how Abdullah had not planned on going and how he had such difficulty getting his visa? I sense somehow that God wanted him to leave."

The two women headed for Zumrat's house, where they were to eat lunch with Zumrat's sister Sofia and her two boys.

"Mama, what did those two men want?" Daniel asked.

"They wanted to talk with Papa," Zumrat said.

This puzzled the nine-year-old boy. "Why are they looking for Papa when he is in Sweden?"

"They don't know he is in Sweden," Zumrat explained. She looked back at the meetinghouse.

"Why did your papa go to Sweden?" Arnold was curious.

"He went to a Christian conference," Daniel told him. "To organize a . . . what is it called, Mama?"

"Evangelical mission," Zumrat answered.

"Yes," Daniel continued, "it's to help our churches work together, Papa said."

"How long has he been gone?" Arnold wanted to know.

"For a week now. He will come home in three more days, Mama told us this morning."

Zumrat soon had the meal ready, and there was a lull in the conversation as the group filled their plates and ate.

"Help yourself to some more potatoes," Zumrat urged her friends. "Soon we will have new potatoes from the garden. Won't they taste good?"

She heard the front door open and all heads turned as rapid footsteps rushed down the hall toward the dining room.

"Sofia, I need to speak to you." It was Aziz, her husband.

Sofia quickly got up and followed Aziz out into the hall. The door closed behind them.

"I pray nothing is wrong," Zumrat said. "I thought Aziz was at his job today. He has to work every other Sunday."

The children were alarmed. They could feel the tension in the air. For a moment, Zumrat felt a wave of panic. First two strange men had come to the meeting place and asked for Abdullah. Now Aziz had left his work and come for Sofia. What was going on?

"Let's pray and ask God to be with Sofia and Aziz. With all of us," Maria corrected herself. "We need to put our faith in Christ Jesus."

"Yes!" Zumrat agreed immediately. The two women and all the children knelt on the dining room floor and began to pray.

Three minutes later, the door opened and Sofia came rushing back in. "We all need to leave this house! Something terrible has happened! They are beating Abdulatip and Olubek!"

They all sprang to their feet. Begzod ran to his mama, who immediately wrapped her arms around him.

"Those men at church!" Zumrat guessed at once. "They were looking for Abdullah!"

"A Muslim man came to the place where Aziz works and demanded to see him," Sofia told them. "He grabbed Aziz and took him to where they had put Abdulatip and Olubek into a room. When he saw them, Aziz said he did not recognize Abdulatip at first, for his face was all puffy and red. Blood was running down his hair."

"Lord Jesus, have mercy on us!" Maria exclaimed. "Have mercy on us and on our children!"

"Come, boys! Aziz says we must go home, for he is sure they will come search for Abdullah here." She pulled her sons to her and hurriedly left the house.

"I will go home," Maria said, beckoning to Arnold. "It is best if we do not stay together. Zumrat, where will you and the children go?"

"Across the city to Abdullah's mother. Perhaps they do not know where she lives."

Almost immediately the house was quiet, the unfinished dinner sitting neglected on the table.

"This is what happens to people who leave the Muslim faith!" The two men pushed Abdulatip and Olubek roughly down the street. The handcuffed men stumbled as they tried to keep their balance.

Crowds of people gathered around the disturbance. *"Allah*

Akbar!" the men shouted. "Only the god of Mohammed is good! Down with foreign gods! Down with the Christians!"

Several young people from the crowd joined in the chants. People threw stones and clods of dirt at the prisoners, yelling derisively.

For the last seven years radical Muslims had been following extremist teachings. As the movement had gained momentum, they had begun lashing out against anyone of other faiths. They had been watching the Christians and had grown alarmed as more and more Muslims embraced Christianity.

"This is what happens to those who leave the Muslim faith! *Allah Akbar!*" The cries grew stronger as more and more men joined the melee.

When the first young boy ran up and spat on Abdulatip, the crowd cheered. Then more and more people ran up, spitting on the helpless men and hitting them with sticks or with their fists.

The two men cried out, "Lord Jesus, help us!" But the yelling crowd drowned out their prayers.

As the speaker talked, Abdullah listened intently. "People in the Philippine Islands are turning to Jesus! Many new churches are starting as people repent and leave their wicked ways."

For Abdullah, it was encouraging to gather with scores of other Christian leaders and hear what God was doing in other countries. It inspired him and fueled his own desire to spread the Gospel.

He hadn't been planning on coming at all, but he had felt the Spirit urging him. Following that leading, he had pursued a passport and visa. It had been worth the hassle to apply for the visa, even if a number of times he had wondered if God was going to open the doors for him to leave Kyrgyzstan.

"It will take days," one officer at the visa office had told him. "You will not be able to leave tonight."

"But I have bought my ticket. My flight leaves at nine o'clock." Abdullah had tried to persuade the man to expedite his application.

"Impossible," came the terse reply.

But somehow God had made it possible. Racing across the city by bus and taxi and arriving at the office only to find it closed had taxed Abdullah's faith. But just as he was turning away in discouragement, someone had yelled, "Hey, sir! Why are you late? I have been waiting with your documents!" And with one last dash to the airport, Abdullah had arrived in time for his flight to Stockholm.

Abdullah's thoughts were interrupted as a man dashed onto the platform and interrupted the speaker.

"The Christians in Kyrgyzstan have been attacked!" he announced. "The Muslims have taken two brothers, and others are being held hostage!"

A murmur of voices rose from the seated men.

Tearfully the man continued. "We received a telephone call from a sister in Kyrgyzstan. They asked that we pray for the believers there, as this morning, after church, they dragged two men away from the meeting and beat them severely. One may be dead, they said. Another group of believers is held hostage inside a house. They will not let anyone enter or leave. Brethren, we must pray!"

Abdullah could not restrain himself. He stood up and with raised hand asked, "In what city?"

The speaker glanced at a piece of paper in his hand. "In Osh," he replied.

"Those are my people! My wife and children! My relatives! Do you know more?"

Shaking his head, the speaker said with compassion. "We were not given any details or names."

The entire group knelt in prayer. Abdullah had no words, only deep inner groanings. "O Lord Jesus, have mercy! Zumrat! My children! My brethren!"

In spite of his terrible anxiety, Abdullah felt the comfort of the Holy Spirit ministering to him. He knew that God could do much more for his family than he could ever do, yet he longed to be with them. "Why did I come? Why did you let this happen when I was gone?" Questions raced through his mind.

"Yet I will trust in you, Lord Jesus. I will put my faith in your strength and power, not in what man can do. Lord, be with them!"

As soon as he could, Abdullah tried to call his house. He let the telephone ring and ring, but there was no answer. It was getting dark by the time he tried to call his mother's house. That line was busy. Later he tried again. He listened as the telephone rang, willing someone to pick up the receiver.

"Hello?"

Abdullah felt a rush of relief as he heard Zumrat's voice. "Zumrat! This is Abdullah! Are you all right?"

Hearing her husband's voice, Zumrat burst into tears. Then, composing herself, she tried to answer his questions.

"We don't know where Abdulatip and Olubek are. The Muslims stayed outside the meetinghouse for several hours after we left, shouting dreadful things. They finally left, but oh, Abdullah, pray for Abdulatip and Olubek! They have been beaten terribly!" Once more Zumrat could not speak as tears choked her.

Then Abdullah heard a commotion in the background. "Someone has just come in," Zumrat informed him. "They are talking about Aziz and Sofia. Oh, please call back later and I will tell you what is happening!"

"Yes," Abdullah agreed. "Zumrat, I love you and the children.

You know I am praying for you!" His own cheeks were wet with tears as he said goodbye.

"Sofia! Whatever has happened?" Zumrat ran to her sister and supported her. An ugly welt marred her cheek, her hair was straggling over her back, and her eyes were red and swollen.

"Take the boys," Sofia gasped. "Oh, boys, pray for your father!" Then she fell into a chair, covered her face, and began weeping loudly. Her sons knelt in front of their mother and wept with her.

"Where is Aziz?" Zumrat asked wildly.

Her question only brought a fresh flood of tears.

"Sofia, remember that Jesus loves you! He knows all about this situation, and He wants to comfort you. Let yourself be comforted by your faith in Him. Remember how Jesus promised us, 'I will never leave you, nor forsake you.' That is His promise to us!" Zumrat whispered words of encouragement to her sister.

It was much later before Sofia could finally bring herself to tell her sad story. The two boys, exhausted, had both fallen asleep on the sofa. Zumrat's children were already in bed and had not heard their cousins and aunt come in. Abdullah's mother and Zumrat listened in horror as the story spilled out.

"They surrounded our house. When they first called Aziz out, I was afraid of what they were going to do with him. The crowd surrounded him and I could hear them yelling and shouting at him. I looked out of the window and saw several men beating him. I called the police, and they said they would send someone out right away. When no one showed up, I called them again and was told, 'Lady, we sent someone.'

"After about thirty minutes I heard Aziz call my name. 'Sofia, bring the children and come out!'

"Oh, Zumrat! I couldn't believe what was happening!" Sofia wept into her hands, quietly, lest she wake her sons.

"I heard voices from the crowd. 'Denounce your Jesus!' Even old women were yelling. I looked at Aziz, and his head was bowed. 'Tell them that you renounce your faith in Christianity and they will leave us alone,' he told me.

"I could not believe my ears! 'No!' I told him. 'I can never do that!'

"The next minutes were terrible. The people kept insisting that I renounce Jesus. 'Do as your husband! Tell us you are Muslim!' Whenever I tried to talk to Aziz, they just yelled and yelled. I could tell by his eyes that he was afraid. 'Just tell them so they will leave us alone!' he kept repeating. Then I saw that a man had grabbed Aziz and was twisting his arm behind his back. I cried out and tried to run to him, but they wouldn't let me. Finally, his face twisted in pain, Aziz cried out, 'She is not my wife! I disown her!'" Sofia was weeping too bitterly to continue.

The two women tried to comfort her. Abdullah's mother rocked back and forth in her own agony. "Lord Jesus, help us! Oh, help Aziz and do not lay this sin to his charge. Have mercy on his soul!"

"He disowned me! He has forsaken his Lord!"

Zumrat told Abdullah everything when he called later. "We still do not know what has happened to Abdulatip and Olubek," she added at the end of her story. "Oh, Abdullah, pray for us! Will we all be destroyed?"

Weeping, Abdullah tried to comfort his wife, but in his own heart, he feared—feared for his wife and children, feared for his relatives and for the church. He felt so helpless, so far away from everyone.

"Heinrich and Zina have been told to stay in their house. There is much talk about them being foreigners," Zumrat told him. "Fear and chaos are everywhere."

Late into the night, Abdullah prayed and cried until he was exhausted. He knew the believers in Osh were doing the same.

Many of the men at the conference prayed with him. The church of Jesus Christ was being attacked.

"To whom can I go? Lord, nothing makes sense, and I cannot understand why this is happening, yet still I trust you. There is no other place to go! I come to you in faith. Though the worst happens, yet I will believe in you!" Then the sad plight of Aziz hit him anew, and with groans of anguish he prayed that his brother-in-law would repent.

Chapter 13

"Zumrat! I am so relieved to hear your voice! How is everyone? Have you heard yet what happened to Abdulatip and Olubek?" The questions tumbled out of Abdullah's mouth as he gripped the telephone receiver.

"It is terrible here!" Zumrat's voice trembled. "Oh, Abdullah, some of the most terrible things are going on!"

Abdullah had been trying to call home from Sweden all that morning. Finally, after ten o'clock, he had been able to get through.

"The first thing we knew about the brothers was last night about three o'clock," Zumrat told him. "We were all still at your mother's house trying to comfort Sofia when a commotion at the door got our attention. It was Olubek. He was carrying your brother, who could not walk."

Abdullah held his breath. "What did they do to him?"

At first there was no answer, then Zumrat managed to say, "They beat him so badly he could barely walk! Oh, Abdullah! His face is swollen, and he has bruises all over his body. They beat him terribly! We don't know if he will live!"

Chills chased each other all over Abdullah's body. He groaned out loud, "O Lord, be merciful to my brother!"

When Zumrat could speak again, she said, "Olubek told us they took them from place to place, shouting loudly to gather attention, then beat them. At one point they took them to a cemetery and began pushing them into an open grave. Olubek says he was certain they were going to bury them alive. They were handcuffed and could do nothing about it. I guess the cemetery keeper's wife heard the commotion and came out and screamed at them. So they pulled them out and dragged them down the road and pushed them into a ditch."

Abdullah's hand ached from gripping the receiver so tightly. He switched the receiver to his other hand.

Taking a deep breath, Zumrat continued. "When Olubek finally got enough strength back, he tried to rouse Abdulatip, but your brother was unconscious. So he picked him up as best he could and carried him here."

"Were they still handcuffed?"

"No. After they left the cemetery, they took the shackles off. I think they thought the men were going to die. Oh, Abdullah! I wish you were here! We don't know what is going to happen to us! The rumors are that the Muslims have declared jihad against all other religions! We are not safe here!"

A sudden inspiration hit Abdullah as he remembered a dear friend in the neighboring country of Uzbekistan. "Listen, Zumrat! As many of you as can, leave immediately for Tashkent. I will call Ahmed and he will find a place for you to stay. Take the children and go! Do you have enough money?"

Zumrat pounced on the idea. "Yes, I have enough!"

"I will counsel with the brethren here," Abdullah told her. "Some are saying I should stay here in Sweden and apply for refugee status. I will pray about it, but meanwhile, buy tickets and, as many of you who can, flee to Tashkent!"

"But what about Abdulatip? He can not travel!"

"Surely Olga will care for her own husband. Even though she is not a believer, she will do her duty."

"I hope so," Zumrat said doubtfully. "She came this morning and hardly said a word. She looked very upset."

"I have to hang up, Zumrat. I will call Ahmed. Go as quickly as you can! I will call you there."

It was good to be back home ... and yet Abdullah was troubled. Easing out of the dark house, he softly closed the door. The warm night air brushed his face.

Abdullah took a deep breath and walked toward the road. It felt good to be outside in the fresh air again after having been cooped up in the house all day. He needed some space to think and pray.

Closing the gate behind him, he put the padlock through the chain and snapped the lock shut, making it look as though it had not been disturbed. Then he walked quickly away from the center of Osh. As he stretched his long legs, his mind cleared.

At first he had not known what to do. Should he stay in Sweden, as some of the brethren there urged him, and appeal to the United Nations for refugee status? "They will help reunite you with your family. You can live here in peace," they had said.

But after earnest prayer, Abdullah had not felt at peace with that option. "I must return to my family," he had told them. "We need to be together." So he had flown to Tashkent and reunited with Zumrat and the children.

True to his word, Ahmed had helped them and given them room in his apartment. But it had been crowded, and after several weeks, Abdullah and Zumrat had decided to return to Osh. The violence had seemed to die down.

As Abdullah walked down the sidewalk, he continued praying.

"Protect us, O Lord, but most of all, keep our faith in you strong! I pray for all of your children." He wept as he thought again how devastating it had been to the church when Aziz had thrown Sofia and the boys out of their home. The Muslims had tortured Aziz dreadfully before he had recanted. Someone had told them that they had held lighted cigarettes against tender parts of his body until he had screamed in pain. "Recant!" they had yelled as they burned him again and again.

When Aziz had finally recanted, he had turned against his wife. "She is not my wife if she does not turn away from her Christ," he had declared as his persecutors cheered.

Aziz now refused to see any of the believers and shouted and screamed at them if they tried to talk to him on the phone.

Walking down the sidewalk into the dark night, Abdullah groaned aloud, his heart burdened. His responsibility for the church weighed heavily on his mind.

Far into the night Abdullah walked, praying and crying out to God. Then he retraced his steps toward home.

"Hsst!" Abdullah stopped as he heard an insistent sound from behind his neighbor's front gate.

"Ranut?" Abdullah spoke softly.

"Come here!" The gate opened and Abdullah could see his neighbor beckoning to him.

Abdullah preaches in Tashkent.

Once inside, Ranut closed the gate. "They were here, asking for you."

"When?" Abdullah felt his scalp prickle.

"This evening, after dark. Four men, and I think they were all armed."

Abdullah's breath caught in his throat. "What did they say?"

Ranut leaned close and said, "They kept asking when you were here last. They asked if anyone had been going in and out since you left the city. I told them nothing. I said I couldn't watch your house. I have my own business, and they need to do their own work. Abdullah, it is dangerous for you to be here! Why did you come back?"

"Thank you, Ranut, for warning me. I must go and see if Zumrat and the children are all right." He hurried to his own gate.

Their house loomed in front of him, dark and still. Now he was extremely grateful to Zumrat for suggesting that, for the first day, they all stay inside and leave no visible sign that they had returned. She had insisted they were being watched.

"Zumrat! Are the children sleeping?" Abdullah asked as soon as he entered the house.

"Yes, why?"

"Get them up and keep them quiet. We must leave! They are watching our house, waiting for our return. They questioned Ranut tonight!"

"Come in!" Heinrich opened the door wide to admit Abdullah and his family. "What is it?"

Abdullah ushered Zumrat and the children into the hall of Heinrich's apartment and waited until Heinrich had locked the door again before answering. "They are watching for us!"

"Come into the living room," Heinrich invited, pushing some cardboard boxes out of the way.

Zina appeared in the doorway that led to their bedroom, blinking sleepily at the visitors. "Zumrat, what is it?" she asked as they embraced.

"Can we spend the night?" Abdullah asked. There was a flurry of activity as the women found spaces for the sleepy children to bed down for the rest of the night.

"Are you going somewhere?" Abdullah asked as he saw the open suitcases on the living room floor.

"Tomorrow we have to leave the city," Heinrich told them. "We received official notice two days ago."

"I didn't know," Abdullah said slowly, "or we wouldn't have come to you for help at such an awkward time. Perhaps we should not have returned to Osh. Our neighbor told me four men were asking for me tonight."

"Armed men," Zumrat added.

"There is rising sentiment against Christians," Heinrich told them. "Have you heard what happened on Monday?"

"No." Abdullah shook his head.

"Do you remember Zinop from the small group of believers in the northern part of the city?" Abdullah nodded and Heinrich continued. "Radical Muslims came to their house and beat her husband for allowing his wife to go to church. They beat him so badly he needed to go to the hospital. After staying in the hospital for several days, he returned home, and once more the Muslims came and harassed him. Everywhere he went, people jeered at him and mocked him for having an unfaithful wife. Well, on Monday something must have snapped, for he took an ax and killed Zinop!"

Zina was weeping softly, and Zumrat gave a cry of alarm. "Killed his own wife!"

Abdullah's thoughts flashed back to the time when he had planned to kill his wife. "O Lord, have mercy!" he groaned.

"He tried to bury her in his backyard, but the neighbors saw blood and the story came out. The police have done nothing about it."

"So the government knows about it and does nothing to stop it," Abdullah remarked. "It's just as we thought. We are not going to get any assistance from the police or the government."

"We are leaving tomorrow to go back to Ukraine," Heinrich continued. "We are Russian Germans, and they came and took our papers and said we cannot stay. It's just an excuse to get rid of us because we are Christians. Since we are not citizens of Kyrgyzstan, we have no choice."

The two couples spent the rest of the night in prayer. The future loomed dark and uncertain before them. In their distress, they turned to God. There was no other place to go. Like Peter, their testimony was, "Lord, to whom shall we go? Thou hast the words of eternal life."

"Things are just getting worse," Zumrat said despondently. "Daniel said today that in school the teachers and the other students constantly mock and harass him. More than one Christian has been beaten, and you know they are constantly looking for you. They want you, Abdullah. Now that Heinrich is gone, they want to get rid of you. They think the church will give up if it has no more pastors."

Abdullah sat quietly.

"We move constantly," Zumrat continued. "Now we live with my mother, but we know we cannot stay. Today she asked how long we will be here." She juggled the sleepless child on her lap.

Zafar was now two. All through the turmoil of that year he had been dragged from place to place along with the other children.

"I wonder if our youngest even knows what a home is!"

"I know," Abdullah said gently, laying his hand on hers. "I am praying for direction, and I still don't know what to do."

Zumrat stroked Zafar's hair. "I'm sorry," she said softly. "I did not mean to complain."

"I went back to our house today and found signs that someone has been there. I saw boot prints in the dirt. I still don't feel comfortable moving our family back there."

Zumrat shook her head. "No, it is not safe."

"Tomorrow morning I am meeting with some of the men at four o'clock to pray for direction for all of us," Abdullah said. "We cannot expect any help or support from the authorities. They just give us vague promises and tell us we are overreacting."

"What happened?" Abdullah asked as soon as he entered the room the next morning. He looked from one brother to the other.

"Galina's husband killed a Muslim!"

"Just last night!"

As the story unfolded, Abdullah's heart grew heavier.

Galina, a young woman who had heard the Gospel story and had repented, was outspoken about her faith. Her husband, Girod, had not embraced his wife's faith, but neither was he against her. "Let her choose whom she wants to serve," he told his neighbors and relatives.

But the radicals had not left them alone. Time and again they had come to their house and harassed the couple. In spite of Girod's protests, they insisted that as long as he did nothing about his wife's beliefs, he was supporting the Christians.

The evening before, a Muslim had once more come to their house, this time with a different approach. "She needs to pay a fine for leaving the faith of our fathers. All Christians will now be fined."

It was nothing new. People posing as officials and trying to extort money from believers had approached more than one Christian. The police just ignored complaints about such harassment.

Girod had met the man outside. "Just wait here," he told him. "I will come back with the fine."

But instead of coming back with money, he came back with an ax hidden behind his back. "Here is your fine!" he yelled, and with a mighty blow he hit the troublemaker on his shoulder.

The man fell to the ground, blood gushing from a severed artery. He bled to death, and as the news spread, a number of Muslims tried to gather support to fight Girod. Like a wild man, Girod brandished his ax. "Come on! I will greet you with the same treatment!" He shouted so wildly that the men left.

"Now perhaps they will leave us alone!" one young man said, looking at Abdullah.

"No, even though Girod is not a Christian, this will not be overlooked," Abdullah predicted. "They may be scared off for a while, but they will be back. In full force."

Their hearts burdened, the men fell to their knees in prayer.

"I saw a vision," one of them said during prayer. "God showed me a vineyard. Clumps of grapes hung from the arbor, and the clump closest to me was heavy and full. Every time we gathered, another grape was missing. Finally only a few grapes were left."

They were all quiet as they reflected on what God had shown them.

"We must flee," Abdullah finally spoke. "I just read in the Bible how Jesus spoke about the end times. He spoke about persecution. When we are persecuted in one city, we are to flee to the next. I see the vision as confirming those verses."

With heavy hearts, the rest agreed.

"We must help those who want to leave," Abdullah continued. "We will not force anyone, but as for me and my family, we will go. Ahmed has invited us to move to Tashkent."

With many tears and prayers, the brethren disbanded. They sensed that the Muslim radicals would gather in greater force and, with the government's silent approval, wreak havoc among the believers. It was time to go.

"What about Maria and Alexander? What will they do?" Zumrat asked when Abdullah returned with the news of the murder and their decision.

"Alexander has already made plans to leave. They are going to Russia or Ukraine. From there, they don't know where they will go."

"If only Alexander would give his heart to the Lord," Zumrat lamented. "I see that Maria has great faith, but how much better if he would believe also."

"Yes," Abdullah agreed. "He hesitates, but he supports her faith and is willing to leave for her sake." His heart ached for his friend, but he knew it must be the work of the Holy Spirit, for many times had he spoken to him about Jesus. "I'm not ready yet," was always the friendly reply.

Chapter 14

"Dildora, could you scoot over a bit more toward your sister? Let's make room for Anya on that bench." Ahmed motioned with his hand.

The room seemed full of children. Actually, there were only nine, but nine children in a not-so-large room can seem quite crowded, especially if they have all been living in the same apartment with their parents and other adults for three months.

"Now, are we ready? One, two, three!

We bless you, oh, Lord Jesus!
We raise our voices to you!
We give our lives into your hands.
Accept our praise this day!"

The childish voices rang out in the small room as Ahmed directed them.

In the other room, Abdullah was trying to study for the next day's worship service. His open Bible lay on the desk, but he stared at the black print with unseeing eyes. Zumrat walked into the room carrying a stack of folded clothes, which she placed on top of a small dresser. As she turned to leave, her foot caught the edge of a mat on the floor, and with a quick twist, she fell onto the bed.

"Are you okay?" Abdullah asked, concerned.

"Yes," Zumrat laughed. "It's good that the bed was right here to catch me! I have to be more careful. There's hardly enough room to even walk in here!"

Resting his head on his hands, Abdullah whispered, "I have been praying and praying about what we should do next. I don't think we should stay here much longer."

"You're not thinking of returning to our house in Osh, are you?" Abdullah could hear the hesitation in his wife's voice.

"No. Things are not settled. Since we know people still enter our house frequently, we also know they are still watching for us. Under Rakhmattula's leadership, the Muslims are getting quite organized. I fear for the lives of any Christians who are still there."

Zumrat smoothed the bed covers with her right hand, tracing the swirled pattern absentmindedly. "What will we do? Ahmed and Tatyana are gracious hosts, but fifteen people living in a four-room apartment? We have been here for over three months!"

"If we could sell our house in Osh, we could maybe buy one here," Abdullah sighed. "As it is, we hardly have any money. We are living on the goodwill of Ahmed and Tatyana." He sighed and ran his hand through his hair. "With the baby coming, we must find a place!"

In the other room, the children continued singing. Then the murmur of voices rising and falling in unison signified that the time of memorization had started.

"If it would not be for the organization here, we would be in much worse shape," Zumrat said with a small smile. "The children are getting good Bible teaching and learning many songs and Scriptures. This will always be a blessing!"

When Abdullah's family, Sofia and her two boys, and Abdullah's mother had first moved in with Ahmed and Tatyana and their three children, it had been exciting for the children. But as the days had turned into weeks, and the weeks into months, they had all realized they needed a schedule to keep things orderly and harmonious.

Now their days were structured from morning until evening. They could not all eat together in the kitchen, so each family ate by turns, with Abdullah's mother sharing meals with her son and his family. The women worked out a schedule to do the cooking and the laundry, and while Ahmed was away at work, Abdullah took over schooling the children. The system was working, but things could not continue this way much longer.

Abdulatip's moans quieted somewhat, but they grated unceasingly inside Abdullah's head. How long could he take this?

He tried to pray, but no words came. All he could say was, "Please, Lord, help us!"

The events of the last few months replayed themselves over and over in his mind. He looked at the silent forms of the boys and hoped they were sleeping. Daniel was on the floor with his cousins, Sherzat and Begzod. The men and boys slept in one room, the women and girls in the other.

He heard the whimpers of their little daughter, Marchamat. She was only a month old and seemed extra fussy. Zumrat tried whatever she could to quiet her baby, but Abdullah felt sure the baby was reflecting the turmoil her mother was going through. *What mother can withstand constant moving from one place to another?* Abdullah wondered. *Four months in Ahmed's apartment, then two months in that other apartment. Only two months!*

It had seemed too good to be true when a woman who had found out about their crowded conditions had offered them her five-room apartment. Five rooms! "No one is living there right now," Anastasiya had told them. "You can stay until . . . well, I don't know how long! How's that?"

That had been just fine—at first. Then it had begun to dawn on Abdullah and Zumrat just what their landlady wanted. Free babysitters.

That was fine with them. They took her three children into the apartment, and eventually the children simply lived there. Anastasiya dumped them off in the morning and often forgot to pick them up in the evening.

Three small children who have not had any training can create havoc in a short time. It took Abdullah and Zumrat's combined efforts to restrain the youngsters and keep their own children in line. After a difficult struggle, the little ones began to benefit from their foster parents' training and started to settle in.

"You know, Anastasiya," Abdullah had told the landlady one rare moment when she showed up, "you can not ignore your children this much and expect a healthy relationship with them. You are their mother. They need you."

The conversation had deteriorated from there, and the final result had been eviction. "I will need the apartment by tomorrow." The note had been brief, but final.

So now they were in this two-room apartment with Sofia and her boys. Ten people.

Plus Abdulatip. Abdullah's brother had never fully recovered from his beating, or from his wife's desertion. Abdullah was not sure which affected Abdulatip more.

Olga had taken care of her husband while he recovered, but she had let him know that if he wanted a future with her, he was to renounce his faith in Christianity and let the men at the mosque know by going there to pray.

"I cannot do that," Abdulatip had said. "I will not deny Jesus!"

When she had cast him out of their house, Abdullah had told him to come to Tashkent. Now he was here, but in physical and mental pain.

Abdullah felt trapped, as if the walls of the room were closing in on him. Outside, the night was dark, and the city noises drifted in through the open window. Inside, the air felt heavy and sticky. Sleep was far away.

Despondent, he prayed, "Lord, I preach to others and tell them to trust in you. Why do I now have this feeling of oppression and helplessness? Why, Lord?"

He drew a deep breath. A faint breeze floated through the window. Finally rising to his feet, Abdullah listened intently, and with a quiet sigh of relief, left the room. Abdulatip was sleeping!

"I am going out," he whispered to Zumrat, who was rocking the baby in the main room where the women and girls slept. "I want to go pray."

With a faint smile, Zumrat nodded. He kissed the top of her head and eased out the door.

The grassy bank beside the river was the perfect place for the weary man to rest. He could hear the water flowing swiftly in the riverbed, fed by mountain springs from high altitudes.

"What have I done?" Abdullah asked, tears threatening to spill out as he lifted his eyes to the heavens. "Lord, did I do wrong to leave Sweden and come back to be with my family? Should I have listened to the brothers there and asked for refugee status?"

Questions tumbled through his weary brain. "Lord, why do you let Abdulatip suffer this way? Oh, keep him from losing his mind! You know he is sick and needs you. You are all he has, God!"

He began to weep. "I'm sorry, Lord! That is all I can say. I'm sorry even for things I don't know I did. I just want you to bless me. Lord Jesus, I need your presence in my life, or I can't make it!"

"What shall we do? What will Sofia and her boys do? What will happen to Abdulatip and my mother? How can we raise our family when we are so destitute?"

It no longer comforted him that they at least had bread to eat. The local Christians shared from their own meager salaries and pantries to help the families who had suddenly come into their midst, but it was not easy for them either. All seemed black and hopeless.

The Lord is my light and my salvation; whom shall I fear? The Lord is the strength of my life; of whom shall I be afraid?

The words came clearly. Had someone spoken to him?

He brought me up also out of an horrible pit, out of the miry clay, and set my feet upon a rock, and established my goings. And he hath put a new song in my mouth, even praise unto our God . . .

Where were these verses coming from? Why did they come so vividly to him now?

Then he heard a chorus of childish voices in his head. The verses the children had memorized while they were staying in Ahmed's house! Those were the verses he had taught the children! Now God was using those very verses to speak to him in his despair!

I will never leave thee, nor forsake thee.

Casting all your care upon him; for he careth for you . . .

Verse after verse sprang into his mind. God was sending him answers!

Abdullah's cries of distress turned into praise. "I don't know how you will do it, God, but I trust you! Though you send me no answers tonight, I cast myself and my family into your care. There is no other place to go! You are the almighty Lord God of heaven and earth! It is to you I turn! I trust in you!"

David. Go see David. The answer came softly.

David? The American Christian they had met?

One Sunday Ahmed's house had been even more crowded

than usual. News had spread about a crippled girl who had been healed and was now able to walk. God had answered Ahmed's prayers and healed the girl, but as Ahmed had explained to the curious peoples who flocked to their house, "We are not miracle workers. We pray to God through Jesus Christ, and He is the one who has healed this sick girl. Listen to what He wants to do for your sick, sinful hearts!"

David had been among the crowd, and Abdullah had been drawn to the tall man. Several other times David had attended their meetings and rejoiced with them as people from the city responded to the Gospel and were baptized.

Go to David. The words came more distinctly.

"That is our situation," Abdullah told the man on the other side of the desk. Ahmed sat in a chair beside him.

David smiled at them and said, "Thank you for coming to me with your needs. I will pray with you about your dilemma."

Their hearts seemed to beat as one as the language school director prayed with them. Then he shook their hands and said, "We will see what God wants to do with this situation. Come back in a week."

"What did he say?" Zumrat asked eagerly as Abdullah entered the apartment. Abdullah told her, ending with, "Then he said, 'Come back in a week.'"

"This is for us?" Dildora asked, traipsing softly from room to room holding Dilnoza's hand. "We can live here?"

David chuckled. "Yes, you may live here. Kind people from America were willing to share with your family so you can have a place to live."

Zumrat's eyes brimmed with tears as she held her baby close.

"There are no beds!" Daniel said coming out of one of the rooms. "No table or chairs, either!"

"Shh!" Abdullah told him quickly. "If God provided us with a place to stay, He can also provide us with the things we need."

"A place to stay," Zumrat agreed. "That's what we were asking for. A place for our family. And God has provided!"

As the family knelt in prayer with David, Abdullah's heart was filled with gratitude. "I know my place is with you, God! I do not know just where all you want to take us, but we thank you for this apartment and dedicate it to you. You have given our hearts a place with you, and for this I am most thankful. Keep my faith strong, Lord Jesus!"

Chapter 15

Four-year-old Zafar ducked under the table and hid in the shadowy spot. He looked at the legs of his brother and sisters as they did their homework. Taking his finger, he tickled a leg. It moved. He tickled it again. It moved again.

He found another leg and tickled that one. This time the leg moved quickly toward him and he had to jerk away to keep from being kicked. He giggled.

"Zafar! I know you are under there." Dilnoza tried to sound stern, but she couldn't keep from laughing. She bent over to peer under the table, but Zafar was gone.

Abdullah laughed with the children. Zumrat cradled their new son, David, while Marchamat, barely a year old, slept in a cradle nearby. It was so good to have a place to call home. True, it was not the same as living in their nice big house in Osh, but they were grateful for what they had. He had been able to find work with some of the local brick masons in Tashkent and was finally earning a decent living for his family.

Things had been rough when they had first moved into this apartment. As Daniel had so bluntly said, there had been no furniture. But little by little, people had donated pieces of furniture, and the landlady had taken them under her wing soon after they had moved in. Whatever she could find she whisked upstairs for "the family with lots and lots of small children." More than once she had sent baskets of food up to their apartment. They finally had a home again.

That evening when the children were in bed and Abdulatip, who lived with them, had gone to his room, Zumrat looked at Abdullah and said, "You know, even though we have a nice place to live, I still often wonder if we will ever return to our house in Osh. What do you think?"

"I wish I knew. Sometimes I think the danger might die down, but every report we get from home says the radical Muslims are still harassing Christians. They have not given up. I'm sure they think they have won a major victory since most of the Christians have left."

Zumrat looked up at her husband. "I sometimes get a feeling that we will not always be able to live here in Uzbekistan. We have only our Kyrgyz passports. We are not registered with the government here."

Abdullah nodded. "I have the same feeling. I remember distinctly when I was praying for a house while we lived with Ahmed that I asked God for a year of peace. I was so weary from being moved from place to place, and I knew it was hard on you and the children. God answered that prayer. We have been living here for more than a year, and we have somewhat of a normal life. We had a good place to live when David was born." He smiled at the sleeping child in Zumrat's arms.

"Let's pray that it will last," Zumrat murmured as she got up to put the sleeping infant to bed.

They heard low moans from the next room, and a look passed between them. Abdulatip must be having a bad evening again.

Abdulatip's mental distress was perhaps the biggest hardship they faced at the moment. It was a daily burden to Abdullah.

Physically his younger brother had recovered from the severe beating, but his heart was still heavy and sore from the trauma he had endured. Plus, every time he tried to contact his wife, he was rudely rebuffed, which caused him great suffering and anguish.

———

"Let me see your passports." The policeman's voice was firm, yet not unkind.

Abdullah pulled the documents from his briefcase and handed them to the officer.

Looking at them, the policeman glanced at Zumrat and the children gathered around the table. He shuffled through all the passports, then checked his notepad.

"You are not residents of Uzbekistan," he said, looking at Abdullah. "You are from Kyrgyzstan. Why are you here? How long have you lived here?"

"Sir, we have lived here for a year." Abdullah answered the last question first. It seemed to be the safest.

"What do you work?"

"I work as a brick mason."

"Do you have a working card?"

Abdullah hesitated only for a moment, then he looked at the officer and answered, "No."

"Where are the papers for the apartment?"

Abdullah provided the documents.

"I will need to look into this matter. I will take your documents back to the office with me."

Panic seized Abdullah. "Sir, where is your office? We need our passports!"

The policeman rattled off a street address, looked at the family around the table once more, then left.

"He had a gun," Zafar said as Abdullah returned to the table.

The older girls glanced at their mother's face. Zumrat sat staring at her plate.

For the rest of the evening, a shadow of uneasiness hung over their home. Was their year of peace about to end?

———————

"Abdullah Jousoupjanov, you and your family must vacate this apartment in three days. Your apartment will be confiscated by the city to be used by an Uzbekistan family waiting for housing. You are illegal residents!"

Fighting off a wave of despair, Abdullah at first could find no words to say. Judgment had been swift. It was the evening after the policeman's first visit, and he had returned. This time, two other officers waited outside in the hall.

Finally Abdullah filled the silence. "Yes, sir. We . . . we will look for another place."

"You must leave the country." The officer's voice was sharp. "You cannot stay in Uzbekistan. Go back to your own country!"

"But we can't!" Zumrat protested, unable to remain quiet. "They will kill my husband!"

"We have no room for troublemakers in our city. You have chosen to follow a foreign religion, and now see where it has brought you!"

So, they had checked out their background in Osh and knew why they were here. Abdullah felt trapped.

"You must get out." The officer turned to leave. "We will be back!" This time he avoided the small faces watching the drama unfolding before their eyes.

"Our passports!" Zumrat said quickly. "You have not returned our passports!"

With a small wave of his hand, the officer ignored her plea.

"Sir, we need our passports, or I can't take my family anywhere," Abdullah said firmly. "We will not be able to leave your country as you ordered."

"Your passports are at the office, and you must . . ." The policeman had turned to address Abdullah as he began to speak, but his voice trailed off when he saw the children moving up behind their mother, eyes wide with fear and uncertainty.

Turning brusquely, he snapped to one of the other officers, "Go to the car and bring my folder."

He stood silently, head bowed, as he waited. Then, taking the folder from the other officer, he pulled out the precious documents and handed them to Abdullah.

With a firm step he left their apartment, closing the door behind him.

"Children, come!" Abdullah drew Zumrat to his side as he spoke. "We will kneel and pray."

Homeless! Driven out! Nowhere to go! Cast away! All these words pounded against Abdullah and Zumrat's consciousness as they poured out their hearts to God. Waves of helplessness and anxiety pounded against the rock of their faith. Yet they prayed—prayed to their Lord Jesus Christ, to whom they had learned to turn in all their trouble.

"Lord, to whom shall we go? You have the words of eternal life!" Once more they put their unknown future into the hands of the living God. "We do not understand, yet we trust in you, Lord God!"

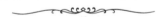

"We can't wait until they throw us out on the street," Zumrat said one evening. Though the officer had not returned after three days, they knew he would make good on his threat in time. "I have a terrible feeling we will be thrown out in the winter."

"I pray and pray," Abdullah told her, "but I have found no answer to our problems. The heavens seem silent to me."

He and Zumrat had agreed to fast and pray together, seeking direction from the Lord. Though this was the fifth day of their fast, Abdullah had no interest in food. He had worked the first several days and then stayed home with the family as he wrestled with his dilemma. That night he left the house again.

The spot beside the river was becoming Abdullah's place of refuge. At night, when the city was quieter and he could leave the house after his brother and the children were sleeping, he went to pray. Here, apart from any distraction, he could talk to God.

"Lord, what do you want us to do?" was his daily prayer. Even though their lives went on as they had for a year, the threat of eviction was very real in their minds. Now, weak in body, his mind was turned toward God. He wanted an answer! Every fiber in his being cried out to know where to take his family. What should he do?

Stretching himself out on the grassy bank, Abdullah gazed into the night. Overhead, the stars twinkled in the moonless sky. Abdullah felt himself shrinking smaller and smaller compared to the vast distance that separated this world from the heavens.

"I am no more than a speck of dust in your sight, O God. Yet I know you care about every thought that troubles me. Help us, Lord! Give us direction! Let us know that you are with us! Give us some confirmation of your presence!"

At first, the faintly glowing light that shimmered in the sky did not attract the praying man's attention. He had often seen the Milky Way and marveled at the innumerable expanse of stars that made the band of light across the dark sky. But this was more. He had read of the northern lights, but he had never seen them. His eyes widened as bands of color began gently moving into place. It was a flag, gently waving back and forth in the heavens!

Abdullah watched in awe. On the top, a wide band of blue appeared, the stars in the corner on the blue background. Then a band of white, and at the bottom, a band of green. Small, narrow strips of dark red separated the bands.

"Lord, are you telling me that we will be able to stay in Uzbekistan?" His heart leaped with hope inside his breast. Perhaps they just had to move to another place!

But another flag was already forming in the night sky. The three bands were very distinct—white on the top, blue in the middle, and red at the bottom.

"God, do you want us to go to Russia?" Perhaps they were to go through Russia to move to Sweden. The believers there had offered them help. Then the colors faded away, and as Abdullah watched, another flag began to take shape—a broader band of blue, then a band of yellow. Simple, yet unmistakable. Ukraine! Were they to go to Ukraine?

It took Abdullah a while to recognize the next flag. Which country flew the flag that, instead of being divided horizontally, was divided into three colors vertically? First blue, then yellow, then red. A faint round circle in the middle of the yellow indicated a seal. Then, even as he wondered, the blue darkened until it was black and the image began to change before his eyes until it was a rapidly changing panorama of waving flags in the heavens.

When the vision faded and Abdullah found himself looking once more into the familiar spangled night sky, he let out a deep breath.

"I do not understand all that you have showed me, Lord, but I thank you for giving me a sign. I know you are here and that you care about me. I will trust in you! Thank you, Lord Jesus!"

"I know we are to prepare to move out of Uzbekistan," Abdullah told Zumrat. "The vision God allowed me to see has made that plain. I have peace in my heart about that."

Zumrat nodded. She understood that the vision her husband had seen was an answer to their prayers and fasting. "I will do all I can to get ready. But," she looked up at Abdullah, "where are we going?"

"I don't know for sure. I just feel that God is telling us to get ready to leave. For now, we will get train tickets for Moscow. From there, we will try to get to Sweden. The believers there have offered to help us."

Zumrat did not say anything. Abdullah lifted her chin and looked deeply into her eyes. "Dear, I know this is hard. I can only do what I feel the Spirit leads me to do. Our lives have changed since we became believers in Christ. Can you trust along with me that, wherever God takes us, we go together as husband and wife?"

Nodding through her tears, Zumrat said, "Yes, Abdullah. When I remember our life before we knew Jesus, I know that in spite of all the uncertain times, we are so much more blessed than we ever could have imagined back then. When I think of your mental struggles and the anguish you endured, I can hardly believe you are the same man! I trust you with all my heart and am willing to follow wherever the Lord leads us."

Abdullah drew his wife to him and wrapped his arms around her. He rested his cheek on her hair and, with tears, began praising God for His boundless love for them.

Perhaps it was because of the size of their family that the officials singled them out from the other people who had fled into Tashkent from Kyrgyzstan. But it might also have been the size of their family that helped Abdullah find the necessary funds to buy the train tickets to travel to Moscow. It definitely helped at the ticket counter when Abdullah requested tickets for himself and his wife and their six children. He was able to buy group tickets at less than half price.

All the details had worked out too. Abdulatip had gone to live with their mother in a small apartment. The officials had not bothered Sofia and her two boys, who were living in an apartment of their own.

"I dare not question why," Zumrat told her husband as the final plans were being made. "I want to be submissive to God's will."

"We will leave in two days," Abdullah had been able to tell the officers when they came to check if they had vacated the apartment. "See, here are our tickets to Moscow."

Then, as Daniel said, they were off like Abraham and his family, not knowing where they went, but with the vivid memory of Abdullah's recent vision as a constant reminder that God would not forsake them as they searched for a home.

Chapter 16

"Lyuba, this man is asking for help," the watchman announced to the middle-aged woman working in the church office.

Lyuba turned to face the two men. Her blue eyes scanned Abdullah's face. Then, frowning slightly, she turned to the watchman. "Why do you bring him to me?"

Viktor shrugged his strong shoulders. "He asked if anyone here can help him with his family."

Looking past the two men toward the door, Lyuba asked, "Family?"

"I have a wife and six children," Abdullah explained politely. "We are looking for a place to stay for the night."

"Where are you from?"

"We are citizens of Kyrgyzstan, but we were forced to leave because we are believers. We are trying to get to Sweden, but so far we have been denied visas, so we came here to St. Petersburg to apply again."

"What do you want in Sweden? Is your wife from there?"

"No. We are looking for a place to live. We lived

temporarily in Uzbekistan, but there, too, we were forced to leave." Abdullah knew his story must sound bizarre to this woman. He looked around the large office and sighed. He ached with weariness. He knew Zumrat was even more tired than he was. He had left her and the children in the square while he had searched out this church building.

"Could we just stay here for the night?" he asked. "We need a place for the children. We have a new baby." He hated to beg, but he was getting desperate.

"We are not a hotel," Lyuba said. "Go to Hotel Stuza. I have heard they have nice rooms."

"We have inquired at hotels, but they are too expensive. We have very little money." There was no way he could afford to pay 160 rubles for a hotel room.

With a shrug, the woman dismissed him. "Like I said, we are not a hotel. We do not have blankets and mattresses."

Abdullah fought against the bitterness that wanted to rise in him. He said no more, but turned and walked outside, followed by the watchman. The huge building loomed behind him, vast and devoid of life.

"Check on the west side of the city," a passerby told him after he inquired where he could get inexpensive lodging for his family. "You'll find a small hotel there."

Abdullah found the hotel as quickly as he could, then went back to the square where Zumrat was trying to entertain the children while they waited.

"I found a room for thirty rubles. It is small, but clean," he told his exhausted wife. Digging out some of their carefully hoarded funds, they purchased bus tickets and left for the hotel.

"I'm so thankful for a place to rest," Zumrat said the next morning. "Last night I was so tired I hardly cared where I was. It's amazing what a good night's sleep can do!"

"Surely the Lord will bless the lady who helped us with this room." Abdullah looked at the children still sleeping on mats on the floor. "She even brought food for the children last evening. As tired as they were, they ate the bread and cheese ravenously. After my experience at the church building yesterday, this woman is an angel."

Then he told his wife about being turned away at the church. "She said they did not have blankets. I would have gladly told her we have our own blankets, but I knew that was not really what she was saying. She did not want us there."

"I think that's how Joseph must have felt when he asked for a room for Mary," Dilnoza spoke up from her blanket on the floor. "He was turned away too."

Zumrat smiled at Abdullah. "And, just as he did for Joseph and Mary, God provided a place for our family."

"Today we will look for another place," Abdullah said. "Even at thirty rubles a night, we cannot afford to stay in a hotel."

"Girls, let's get the blankets and roll them together. We need to make tight bundles again, for we don't know how long we will need to carry them with us." Zumrat began planning.

"Will we try to go to Sweden?" Daniel wondered, sitting up and rubbing his eyes. "I hope we can find a place to live soon."

Shaking his head, Abdullah said, "I will check again at the visa office in Moscow, but the officer was quite firm that we cannot hope for a visa soon. He said things have changed since the Soviet Union broke up and the countries became independent."

"But you got a visa to go to Sweden," Daniel said, puzzled.

Abdullah did not want to tell him that, when he had gone to Sweden, he had been asking for only one visa. Now they were asking for eight visas—a much larger hurdle.

"If God wants us in Sweden," Zumrat said confidently, "He will make a way for us to get there."

Abdullah was making a small pile of blankets on the floor.

Zumrat watched curiously as he folded them together and tied a piece of string around them. "What are you doing?" she asked.

"This is a bundle for the people at the church where I asked for help yesterday. I feel we should donate some of our blankets to them."

"Were they poor?" Dildora asked. "Like us?"

"Sometimes people are poor and don't know it," Abdullah said simply. "I am praying that they might become rich."

"Oh, good!" Daniel laughed. "Now we don't have to carry so many bundles around. People always stare at us when we arrive with our huge bundles."

Abdullah smiled at his family. "Well, we are on a journey. That is plain for all to see."

"A journey to where, Papa?" Dildora asked. "Where are we going?"

"A journey of faith," Zumrat answered, both for her daughter's sake and her own.

"What did she say?" Daniel asked as Abdullah walked out of the church without the bundle. They were waiting once again in one of the many squares in St. Petersburg.

"She wasn't there, so I gave the bundle to the watchman and asked him to deliver it to her."

"Was he surprised?" Dilnoza asked.

"I think so. I told him that we hope the next time someone comes and needs a place to stay they will help them and let them use the blankets. He seemed embarrassed, so I told him I was not trying to make him feel bad. But I did tell him I believe Jesus comes to people unawares sometimes and asks for something. If we are not willing to help, it's as though we are turning Jesus away."

"Did you preach to him, Daddy?" Daniel asked with a grin.

Abdullah chuckled. "I guess I did, didn't I?"

The train trip to Moscow was short compared to the six-day journey from Uzbekistan to St. Petersburg. In less than eight hours the family arrived at the Moscow train station.

"Yes, yes, of course you are welcome to stay in the church building!" Iosef told them. "It's not quite finished, but you may stay."

Abdullah breathed a sigh of relief, thanking God for directing him to this place. But his heart sank when he saw the place they had been given for refuge. Thankfully, most of the windows and doors had already been installed in the brick building, but the wind blew in along the rafters. The summer days were ending and the nights were becoming chilly.

"Thank you," Abdullah said gratefully to their host. After the rebuttal in St. Petersburg, at least this man was willing to help.

"I live in a small apartment myself," Iosef told him. "My wife and I have three children. I wish I could invite you to stay at our house, but there is simply not enough room. We will see what we can do to help you. How long will you be in Moscow?"

What could he say? Abdullah had no idea. "We are trying to get to Sweden," he began, "but we can't get visas."

Iosef's brow wrinkled. "What brings you here? You told me you were from Kyrgyzstan."

So Abdullah told their story once again.

"Wow! You really are on a journey to nowhere," Iosef said, looking keenly at the family. "Well, how are you fixed for food? Can I get you something? There's a bread shop right around the corner. I'll go get some bread for you." He chucked Zafar under his chin and left.

"I almost wish you wouldn't have given those blankets away,"

Zumrat said, tucking her coat around Marchamat. "Are you sure they will even use them? It's getting chilly."

"I hope it doesn't appear that I was trying to heap coals of fire on that lady's head," Abdullah said slowly. "I really wasn't, but I felt the Spirit telling me to give that bundle."

Zumrat nodded. "I won't complain. I know you wouldn't do it for a wrong reason."

The next night the wind blew even colder, and the unheated building was cold and drafty. Zumrat tried to get all the children to sleep close to each other. The mattresses Iosef had brought helped, and the next day he brought more blankets. Another brother from the church brought a small heater, but it did little to take the chill out of the air.

Little David suffered the most. As hard as his mother tried to keep him warm, he caught a cold, and his nose was stuffy. He became fretful and developed a fever. Some of the other children soon became sick, and even Abdullah felt ill.

"We must get you out of here!" Iosef said when he stopped in one day. "You're freezing in here! I will go immediately to a hostel and arrange for you to stay in one of their rooms. It may be small, but at least it will be warm."

"Please hurry," Zumrat urged, fighting tears. "My baby is very sick."

"We now know you are true believers," Iosef apologized. "I must admit that at first I doubted your story, for there are many who try to get help with sob stories. But we have watched you for these two weeks, and I can tell you are genuine. Please forgive me."

Abdullah smiled. It was hard for him to remain silent, but he merely said, "God is good to us."

That night they slept in a warm house. No one minded that

they were all in one room. They were warm! The children crowded around the radiator and luxuriated in the heat.

When the kind woman who ran the hostel came to check on them and brought bowls of hot soup, they were ecstatic. "Let me hold your baby while you eat," she said to Zumrat. Taking the baby, she exclaimed, "Oh, my! He is burning with fever!"

Later she returned with blankets and warm water and helped Zumrat bathe David's hot little body. The other children snuggled into the blankets on the floor. Finally they were warm!

"I didn't know it was possible to work in such cold weather," Abdullah told his coworker, Ivan.

"This is Moscow!" laughed Ivan, a ruddy, cheerful man. "Moscow may be cold, but there are plenty of jobs here. Now in Odessa, in southern Ukraine where I come from, we don't have such cold winters. But right now jobs are scarce. That's why I came north."

Once more Abdullah had found employment as a mason. As Ivan said, jobs were plentiful in Moscow, and it was rewarding for Abdullah to be able to earn an income for his family.

Now they felt a close relationship with the church. Iosef was a pastor with a burden for the people of his city, and he spent long hours teaching and preaching. When he found out Abdullah was ordained, he often asked him to help in the ministry and preach at their services. Even though they were not Russians, Abdullah's family felt at home with the believers there. But the cold! They just were not used to the penetrating cold of the north.

"Oh, Odessa! Land of warmth and sunshine!" Ivan sang one cold day in May. "There it is warm already like summer, and here we hardly know winter is over! Oh, Odessa!"

Abdullah grinned. "You left Odessa to come here for work, so not all is warmth and sunshine there."

Sobering, Ivan said, "You know what? My father told me on the phone that a big construction job is coming up that will provide work for bricklayers for months. I asked him to apply for me. Perhaps soon I can go home!" His merry eyes sparkled at the very thought.

"How are the churches there?" Abdullah asked.

"Like ours here," Ivan said. "In fact, we have more than one church like this one. We have many believers, and our pastors are very active. You would fit right in."

Abdullah picked up a brick and deftly spread mortar on it. With a swift movement, he placed the brick on top of the wall.

"You should come with me," Ivan said, watching his companion work. "You could easily get a job if that building gets under way."

"You go first and get the job," Abdullah said. "I will pray about it. It might be a good idea. None of our efforts to get to Sweden have paid off. We are always turned down when we apply for visas."

Then David got sick again. His small body grew feverish, and nothing Zumrat did made his temperature go down.

"He must stay in the hospital," the doctor said, examining the infant. "How old is he?"

"Seven months," Zumrat said.

"Has he been sick a lot?"

"Yes. All winter he has been sickly. He is not used to the cold."

The doctor stood up and called for a nurse. "Put the child in the pediatric ward." Then he gave detailed instructions for his care.

"Perhaps we should go to Odessa." Abdullah brought up the subject that evening as he stood beside Zumrat watching their son struggling to breathe.

"Why Odessa?" Zumrat lifted her red eyes toward Abdullah.

"Ivan called and said the building project has started. He is sure I can find work there."

Looking at her sick son, Zumrat said, "At least it would be warmer there. Maybe the children would not get so sick."

Even in July, Zumrat wondered if it ever warmed up in Moscow. She felt cold most of the time. Perhaps in a warmer climate her baby could get better. "Let's pray about it," she whispered. "I am ready to go if you are."

Once more Abdullah took time off work to fast and pray. He was needed at home anyway, for Zumrat stayed with David in the hospital, and they did not want to leave the smaller children alone while the older ones went to school.

"I must know, God," Abdullah prayed. "Please give us a sign! Do you want us to find another place to live?"

They had been in Moscow for almost a year now, with no indication that they would ever get visas to travel on to Sweden. And Abdullah was not sure what he would do even if they got to Sweden. Could they live there?

How long could they live here in Moscow before they were kicked out? Would the Russian government be any more sympathetic to their plight than the Uzbek government? Hardly. They just hadn't found them yet. Someday they would have to appear before government officials and try to get registered for some reason or other. They could not live in the hostel forever.

Abdullah knew their days in Moscow were numbered. All former Soviet countries—and many European ones—required registration. They could not legally rent or buy property or enroll their children in school until they had registered with the local government. Since they could claim no relatives in the city and no company had sent him a formal invitation to move there for a job, he knew the chances of their application for registration being accepted were slim.

The room seemed ever smaller. They had moved the big bookshelf across the corner to make a bedroom for himself and Zumrat, but the children all had to sleep on the floor and take up their mattresses every morning. And the children were getting older. Daniel was already twelve, and Dilnoza and Dildora were ten and nine. They really did need more room.

Then Abdullah remembered his vision. The Ukrainian flag! It had been etched against the night sky.

"God, if you provide money for the tickets, I will take my family to Odessa!"

When he told Zumrat, she said, "The doctor told me that David will be able to leave tomorrow. Look how well he is!"

"Then we will go and see about the tickets," Abdullah told her. "If God provides tickets we can afford, we will make plans to leave."

The next day, Abdullah and Zumrat left the children in the care of the woman who ran the hostel and went to the train station.

"We're too late," Abdullah said. "They have closed the ticket windows for lunch."

"No, I see someone inside," Zumrat said and walked up to the window.

Even though the closed sign was plainly visible, the lady asked, "How may I help you?"

"We need tickets for our family to Odessa, please."

"I cannot help you. There are no tickets available."

Perhaps she is a cleaning lady, Zumrat thought. She hesitated, then turned away.

After checking at the other windows, which were also closed, they walked past the window where Zumrat had seen the woman.

"Lady!" someone called, and Zumrat turned to see the woman beckoning to her. "Come here. You said you wanted to buy tickets to Odessa? How many are going?"

Zumrat glanced up at Abdullah and said, "Eight. We have six children."

The woman gasped. "Six children! Oh, I don't know if that's possible. I found an overnight car that leaves late this evening, but for eight? Let me see." After a few clicks on the keyboard, she frowned at the screen.

"If you leave your passports with me, I'll see what I can do, but I can't promise anything!"

"But do you have tickets?" Iosef asked as Abdullah told the pastor that they planned to leave for Odessa that very evening. "Does Ivan know you are coming?"

"Yes. I called him, and he invited us to stay with him until we can find a house," Abdullah told him. "The tickets will be ready when we get to the train station. I say that by faith." He told Iosef what had happened.

Yes, the tickets were there, and once more God had given them tickets at a rate far below the going price. Abdullah was once again blessed as he felt God's hand guiding them.

"God bless you and keep you! May He make His face to shine upon you!" Iosef prayed for their family as they said farewells. About twenty believers from the church had come to the train station to see them off. With songs and prayers, they encouraged them.

On through the night the train made its way south, carrying Abdullah and his family toward Odessa.

Chapter 17

"Welcome! Welcome!" Ivan greeted Abdullah warmly and shook hands with Zumrat and the children. "How is the baby?"

"He's better, praise the Lord!" Abdullah's heart was warmed by his friend's hearty welcome. The train trip had been long and tiresome, but they were relieved to find a ready welcome and a place for them to live this time. The August sun warmed them as they left the train station, following Ivan with their few suitcases containing their clothes.

"My house has two extra rooms, and you can live there for now," Ivan explained. "I have also inquired about work, and the need is great for brick masons. You can begin working as soon as you are settled."

Ivan's village farmhouse was typical for Ukraine. A head-high wooden fence surrounded the yard, and the one-story whitewashed house stood solidly in the center. All around the house were fruit trees, and a big garden grew luxuriantly in the back.

"Here is your portion of the house," Ivan told them. He pushed open a door that opened off the front entry and ushered them inside.

"Oh, thank God!" Zumrat said quickly. "Such nice, big rooms! Oh, how much better than our cramped rooms in Moscow!"

Ivan's wife Luda joined them, carrying their one-year-old daughter. "Welcome!" she greeted Zumrat warmly. "I apologize for not having furniture for you, but we moved in here ourselves just a year ago." She laughed as she added, "We hardly have more than a bed and table, as you will see."

"Thank you so much for giving us these rooms! You can't imagine how grateful we are to be welcomed and given a place to live. This is like home already!"

"I have fixed a meal for you," Luda said, smiling at the children. "I know you all are tired, but when you have cleaned up you can come eat with us."

Ivan showed them the back porch, where water was piped into a sink. "You can wash up here. In the summer it's warm enough to take showers over there." He pointed to the corner of the back porch.

"The weather is so beautiful here!" Dilnoza said in wonder.

"Yes, we have lots of warm weather. In the winter we occasionally get snow, but nothing like Moscow!" Ivan laughed.

As Luda had told them, the two rooms were bare of furniture, but she brought blankets to make a bed for little David. It was warm enough that Zumrat could take most of her baby's clothes off and let the small boy enjoy stretching out on the floor.

"We'll leave you alone. As soon as you are ready to eat, come on over," Ivan told them as he and his wife left.

"Oh, children, come!" Abdullah told his family, drawing Zumrat to his side. "We will kneel and thank God for giving us this place to live—for giving us a home!"

Their arrival coincided with the summer harvest. And what a harvest it was! Watermelons, apples, pears, grapes, and all manner of vegetables were bestowed upon the newly arrived family. As Ivan's church learned of their plight, they opened their hearts and shared generously. Even though they only had mattresses on the floor for beds and an old table, they felt truly blessed.

The leader of the church came and introduced himself to them. "We welcome you, brother!" Elia said warmly. "Ivan has told us of your difficulties, and we are happy to do all we can to make your family comfortable."

Abdullah was almost moved to tears by their kindness. "We feel so privileged," he told the elderly man. "We bless God for your church. It is more than we ever anticipated."

"We are glad to help," Elia said simply. "In fact, we have a warehouse of used clothing that has been donated by kind people in America for the believers here, and we want you to come and pick out anything you need for your family."

Zumrat found much-needed clothes for their growing children. However, she was very careful to take only what they needed.

"Take more! Why are you taking so little?" Elia wondered, his forehead wrinkling in dismay.

"This is plenty," Zumrat told him. "We have found it is not good to have too many possessions, for it makes it difficult to take our things with us when we move from place to place."

"But," Elia protested, raising his hand, "you can stay with us here in Chevchenkova! We are not far from Odessa, and Abdullah can find work. You are welcome to make this your home."

After a moment of silence, Abdullah reminded him, "I have not yet registered with the police. We do not know how long we will be allowed to stay."

This sobering thought chilled him even as he spoke. He and Zumrat didn't speak about it much, but it was on their minds constantly.

With a wave of his hand, Elia said, "Now don't worry. We'll pray about it, then I will go with you to the police station. You are here at our invitation. Surely that gives you the right to live here! You have a good job, right? We can help you, and perhaps soon you can buy your own house. You will need more room for your growing family."

———

"It would be easy to plan to stay here for the rest of our lives," Zumrat told her husband one evening. "The climate is so nice, and the gardens do so well. It's almost like paradise!"

"Yes," Abdullah agreed. "The church has welcomed us with open arms. I feel at home with the believers, and our children are making friends. Maybe this is where God has planned for us to make our home."

"I do miss our family and friends in Uzbekistan and Kyrgyzstan," Zumrat said reflectively. "It is good to know that your mother and Sofia are settling in nicely in Tashkent. How was Abdulatip the last time you spoke with him on the phone?"

"Still heavy in his heart. I pray that somehow he will be completely healed and have his spiritual health restored."

"When will you register?" Zumrat asked, bringing up the subject Abdullah had been trying to ignore.

"I know I should," he said slowly. "But it almost seems better not to know than to go and be rejected. I know it is weak of me, yet I fear being told to leave this place."

"Will it put Ivan and Luda in a difficult position if the authorities find out we are living here?" Zumrat did not want to bring trouble to their gracious hosts.

Abdullah nodded slightly. "Yes, I think it might."

———

"These passports are no good." The officer peered at Abdullah through the glass window that separated them. "They are Kyrgyz passports, and for your youngest son you only have a birth certificate."

Clearing his throat, Abdullah tried to explain. "Sir, we had to leave our home. My life was in danger, so we fled our country. We have no place to go!"

"That is not our problem," came the unsympathetic reply. "That is your problem."

With a sinking heart, Abdullah took his useless papers and turned away.

"We will not give up," Elia told them that evening. "We are in contact with a mission in Kiev, and we will write to them. They can intercede for you with the Bureau of Foreign Affairs. Come, I have the address. You write the letter and we will send it."

Abdullah hesitated. "What is this mission? How can they help us?"

"This mission is funded by foreigners and helps believers all over Ukraine, Moldova, and Russia. They have connections with head government officials and are instrumental in helping the churches. They have provided funds for many churches to build houses of worship."

Eagerly Elia continued. "If we present your case to them, I think the mission directors would take an interest in our congregation here and perhaps even help us buy some land so we could build a house of worship."

Something did not seem right to Abdullah. "You want us to write a letter so this mission will recognize your church and give you financial aid to buy land and build a church house?"

"Well, the primary reason would be to get you registered here in Ukraine, of course. You do need a place to live!"

Shaking his head slightly, Abdullah said in a puzzled tone, "I don't know how this mission could help. They are not officials in the Foreign Affairs Office."

Elia grew slightly impatient. "They have friends there. Connections. That's how it is done, you know. Everything is done by having connections with the right people. A situation like yours is just what we need to establish those connections."

"I want to pray about this," Abdullah said. "I don't have a clear leading in this case."

"There's little else you can do," Elia reminded him somewhat shortly. "You need a place to live. Who else can help you?"

Looking at the older man, Abdullah told him softly, "We want a place for our family to live. My wife suffers from not knowing if we have a home or not. The children suffer too, for they feel the uncertainty of our lives. But we also know God will give us a place to live whenever it is His will. In spite of my disappointment in not getting a registration for me and my family, I will still trust in God's provision."

Elia made no immediate answer. Then he looked at Abdullah and said somewhat sharply, "I sensed pride in you when I took you and your wife to pick out clothes from the warehouse. You only took a few pieces and left many good articles of clothing behind. I urged you to take more, but no, you were too good for used clothing! Now I ask you to do something that might help us, and you refuse! Brother, I ask you to examine your heart and see if you do not harbor the sin of pride in your life!"

Far into the night, Abdullah and Zumrat prayed and cried out to the Lord. "God, I do want to know if I am proud! You know our hearts, and we lay ourselves before you in humility. Show us ourselves! I know it says in your Word, 'The heart is deceitful above all things, and desperately wicked: who can know it?' I give my heart to you and beg you to show me any wicked way there might be in it." This blow was one of the hardest that Abdullah and Zumrat had endured in their wanderings.

At first it had truly seemed like paradise in Chevchenkova. Work was good, food was plentiful, and the people had all been so friendly. Now, as the summer was ending and the chillier days of autumn lay icy fingers over the land, life became more difficult for Abdullah and his family.

David, barely a year old, was still sickly and fretful. Marchamat, too, seemed to be ill frequently, and even though they used heavy blankets at night, the unheated rooms became more and more like the unheated church had been in Moscow.

But even more chilling was the attitude from the people at church. Elia no longer asked Abdullah to preach, and he sensed a coldness from many of the brothers. He still heard a lot of talk about the need for a proper church building and complaints of having to hold meetings in a house. At times it seemed as though the men talked about it specifically when they knew he was listening to their conversations.

Even Ivan and Luda seemed to change in their attitude toward the large family that lived in their house. The two women shared the same kitchen, as Ivan had told them they were welcome to do, but Zumrat felt she was in the way and hated to ask Luda for any favor.

"It is hard for two families to live under the same roof," Abdullah acknowledged to his wife one evening after the children were under their blankets. "We must never forget the kindness they showed to us when we arrived. Perhaps it is time to look elsewhere for a place to live."

Abdullah had returned to the police station to reapply for registration, and this time he was faced with hostility. "You must leave!" the officer told him bluntly. "You have no right to live here in Ukraine!"

<hr/>

"A big, healthy boy," Abdullah said with a large smile as he placed the newborn baby beside his wife. "And in a hurry to meet his family!"

Zumrat held out her arms, and Abdullah placed the baby beside his mother. Tears of joy trickled down Zumrat's flushed face.

A knock on the door interrupted them. "Come in," Abdullah called.

"Oh, what can I do to help?" Elena asked, bustling inside and taking off her coat. Then, her mouth open in surprise, she tiptoed softly over to the bed.

"You already have your baby?" she asked, holding her hand over her mouth. With wide eyes she looked at Abdullah. "You . . . you helped? No one else was here? You didn't go to the hospital?"

Abdullah laughed softly. "There was no time to go to the hospital. When we realized our son was about to be born, we knew it was better to stay right here than to try to rush to the hospital."

"But how did you know what to do? I mean, certain things must be done!"

"God was with us," Abdullah reminded her. "When we knew the birth was imminent, we prayed, and God heard our prayers. Everything went smoothly."

"Oh, yes, I know you are believers! I still have my mother-in-law today as proof of that! When you prayed for her and she became better almost immediately, I knew God had heard your prayers. Remember, that is why you are here with us today!"

"Yes, and we are so thankful to you and Nicolai for providing a warm place for my family to live," Abdullah said gratefully.

Ivan's unheated rooms had been no place for their family, and after Nicolai's mother's quick recovery, Nicolai and Elena had insisted that they move into rooms in their heated house.

"Plus," Abdullah had told Ivan, "it is better for us not to live in one place for a long time, as we still are not registered here."

Ivan had agreed, so with their few belongings, they had moved again—to another temporary place, where Johann was born.

"Come to Moldova. We are a poor country, and perhaps you can become registered there," Mikhail Ches invited Abdullah. "We will find a place for you to live, and I'm sure a brick mason can find a job in Chisinau."

Abdullah had warmed immediately to the sincere pastor from Moldova when he had visited Ukraine and held meetings at the local church. When Mikhail had heard of their plight, he had spoken sincerely to the homeless man. "Pray about it. I want you to know that if God leads you to Moldova, we will welcome you."

Abdullah nodded. He knew they could not stay in Ukraine much longer. Somehow the government would find out they were still living here and once more force them to leave. It would be better to go before they were expelled.

Zumrat said very little when Abdullah asked her to pray with him about leaving Ukraine. "To Moldova?" was her only question.

But Zumrat's heart was heavy as she once more packed their few belongings and prepared to leave. Leave for where? Another country that would only possibly give them a place to call home? When, oh when, could they find a permanent place of refuge?

Come unto me . . . and I will give you rest. Jesus' words came to the weary woman's heart as she prayed. *Your rest is not in where you live. Your rest is not in having a permanent place in this world that you can call your home. Your rest is in me! Come, weary one! Come to the arms of the Saviour and I will give you rest for your weary heart! Come!*

Zumrat felt lifted out of her body and into the spirit world as she cried out to Jesus. His loving arms carried her up and away to the place where her Lord was waiting for her. There her strength was restored, and she found rest for her weary heart.

"Oh, thank you, Jesus, my Lord and Saviour! Thank you for this wonderful experience with you!"

Her faith strengthened, Zumrat gladly accompanied her husband and children to the train station once more and boarded the car to go to yet another country. Like Abraham, they set out not knowing where they went, searching for an earthly home. But also like Abraham, their hearts were set on a city not made with human hands.

Chapter 18

Zumrat lay in the hospital, staring at the ceiling. A fine crack in the plaster reached out from the corner and zigzagged into the center of the room. She studied the crack, trying to concentrate on something to ease the dull pain. She moved restlessly on the hospital bed, shifting her weight to one side. Why was this baby so slow in coming?

She focused on the crack again. First it went one way, then changed directions and went back the other way again. Five times it changed directions before it ended close to the light bulb in the middle of the room.

The hospital in Moldova had obviously been built many years before, and modernization had only reached a few of the rooms. Most of the interior was drab and in desperate need of updating.

Once more her eyes followed the crack. Anything to keep her mind occupied.

She sighed deeply. She was so tired. Tired physically, for she had experienced more difficulty with this pregnancy than any of the other seven children, but also tired in spirit.

That crack could represent our lives, Zumrat thought.

Five times they had moved to another place, looking for a place to call home. First, of course, they had lived in Kyrgyzstan, where they had married and built their house and where their first four children had been born. There they had begun their journey with the Lord Jesus Christ.

Zumrat remembered her house with pleasure. Spacious rooms, a big kitchen, and plenty of room for their entire family. Even now, with their eighth child coming soon, that house would have been plenty big enough. It had been warm in the winter and cool in the summer. Abdullah had had a good job, and life had been good to them. They had enjoyed the fellowship with other believers, and as they had continued to spread the Gospel, more and more people had come to know the Lord. Yes, it had been a wonderful time in their lives.

Her eyes followed the first line to where it changed direction. That line represented their flight into Uzbekistan—the beginning of their wanderings. She remembered the crowded, precisely scheduled days in Ahmed's apartment. She thought of all the Bible verses and songs her children had learned there and was grateful for the fruit that time of testing had yielded.

She relived their move into the next apartment, where Marchamat and David had joined their family. After a lengthy stay they had been evicted. Why them? Why did the others get to stay and make a life in Tashkent?

Zumrat firmly pushed those thoughts away. Asking why was not going to help.

As she followed the zigzag line across the ceiling, her thoughts drifted to their long train journey to St. Petersburg, then on to Moscow and their stay in that enormous city.

The next line signified their journey to Ukraine, near Odessa. With fond memories Zumrat thought of the plentiful harvest and the warm climate. There the children had gotten over their continued sickness, and Johann had been born. She remembered how she had hoped they could make their home in that community.

Now it was 1996, and they had been in Moldova nearly two years. They had enough space in the three-room apartment, and Abdullah had been able to get work almost immediately. They enjoyed the spiritual nourishment from the church, but they still had not been able to gain any legal status.

"Sorry, but you have no relatives in Moldova, and there is no reason to accept you as citizens." The official reply had come a year and a half after they had applied. Once more their hopes were dashed.

Zumrat was not sure she had any hopes left. Especially today, when her body was so tired and her mind wandered so. Why did the pain persist? What was happening to her?

Abdullah found his wife in this foggy state of mind when he came to the hospital. Before he could speak to her, she drifted into unconsciousness.

"There are complications," the doctor told Abdullah vaguely. "She needs a C-section."

Abdullah answered quickly. "Go ahead and operate. She is very sick and weak. I tried to talk to her and she did not answer. Something is very wrong."

"The first opening is at noon today. The operation will cost $200," the doctor told the distraught man bluntly.

"I ... we ... uhmm," Abdullah tried to think quickly. "Prepare for the operation. I will be back as soon as I can."

He did not want to tell the doctor they did not have $200. All his wages went toward food for the children and rent for the apartment. It was expensive to buy food for his large family, and even with help from the believers, he did not have $200 to pay for an operation.

The older children were in school, and the younger ones had been staying with people from the church for the past week, so the apartment was empty when Abdullah stumbled in the door and sank to his knees.

"Help us, Lord! How can we get the money? I cast our needs before you and plead that you spare Zumrat and our baby! You know I need her, Lord! How can I take care of the children you gave us if my wife dies?"

He pushed the thought away. "I will trust in you. Always, when I have cast myself on your mercy, you have heard my prayers. Once more I will trust in you. Even if you take Zumrat home to be with you in heaven, I will trust in you. I give our lives into your care, my Lord and my God!"

In his desperation, Abdullah turned to the God he had learned to trust, and the Lord gave peace to his trusting soul. Communion was sweet as Abdullah waited.

The harsh jangle of the telephone broke in on Abdullah's prayers.

"This is Viktor. I heard Zumrat is in the hospital, and the Lord laid it on my heart to call you and see if there is anything you need. I want to help you."

Abdullah's heart leaped. He knew Viktor from the fellowship, though there was no special connection between the two.

"How did you know?" Abdullah could not help asking. "Zumrat needs a C-section, and the doctor wants $200 to perform the operation."

"Look, I'm close to the hospital right now," Viktor replied, his mind racing to form a plan. "I'll meet you in the front lobby with the money in ten minutes."

"Lord Jesus," Abdullah prayed in amazement, "how merciful you are!" He left the apartment, praise bubbling from his heart. God had once again marvelously answered! Oh, he prayed it was not too late!

"Zumrat, we have a baby girl!" From somewhere far away, Zumrat heard Abdullah's voice. "God has given us a baby girl!"

She wanted to tell him she was glad, but a heavy weight seemed to be pressing on her chest and she could not speak.

"Open your eyes," another voice commanded. Then someone shook her shoulder. "Lady, open your eyes."

She could not. She was too weak. Once more she slid into unconsciousness, oblivious to her husband's tears as he battled in prayer for her life.

The light was faint at first, but gradually became brighter. Through half open eyes, Zumrat tried to focus on the light. Was it the sun shining through the hospital window? No, the window was on the opposite wall. This light was moving slowly, coming toward her. Something stood in front of the light—a man. Was Abdullah there?

The figure became plainer. The light was no longer behind the figure—the figure *was* the light. Zumrat gazed in awe as the man came closer, his flowing robe shining.

"Jesus!" Zumrat heard her own voice whisper weakly. "You have come for me! I am ready!"

As Jesus reached toward her, she tried to lift her hand, but could not. Zumrat felt His strong hands clasp her own. She wanted to tighten her grip, but she still could not move. She lay helpless, gazing into that wondrous face. His loving eyes returned the gaze.

Strength flowed into her from His hands. Power surged through her body, and she could breathe again. A wonderful feeling swept over her, and, as marvelous as the experience was, she found herself drifting into sleep. She closed her eyes. The last thing she remembered was feeling the hands of Jesus on her own.

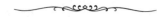

"Thank God you are better!" Abdullah breathed as he knelt beside Zumrat's bed and took her hands in his own.

Zumrat smiled. "Jesus came to heal me," she said simply. She was amazed that she could talk. She was still very weak, but the strength she had felt in her vision with Christ was still with her.

Smoothing back her hair, Abdullah said, "I believe it. You were so weak that I thought you were dying. But God gave you back to us! My dear wife, I love you! I am so grateful that you did not leave me and the children!"

Zumrat told him about the shining figure coming into her room. "He was right here," she said, looking at the side of the bed. "I felt his hands on mine! I was touched by the healing hands of the Lord Himself!"

Then she remembered. "How is the baby? It's a girl, right?"

Abdullah said gently, "She is very weak. So tiny, too. When you are stronger, we will go see her in the incubator." Then his voice grew firmer. "She is in God's care. We will trust the same God who kept you with us to care for our daughter and give her strength."

So they prayed together and committed their tiny infant into the hands of the Lord.

"It's David," Zumrat told her husband. "He's much worse."

Abdullah sat up in bed. He blinked his sleepy eyes several times, then got out of bed and joined his wife beside the three-year-old's bed.

"Feel his forehead. He's all hot and feverish," Zumrat said, trying to pick up her son.

"Let me," Abdullah said. Gathering his son into his arms, he felt the fever burning through his nightclothes.

"We have to take him to the hospital," Abdullah decided. "He is very sick. How are Johann and little Zoumrad?"

The three youngest had been fretful the day before, but at the time they had been mostly concerned about the tiny premature baby. "They are sleeping," Zumrat said. "They still feel a little feverish, but not like David."

While Abdullah dressed, Zumrat woke Dilnoza. "We're taking David to the hospital," she told her sleepy twelve-year-old daughter. "I don't know when we'll be back, but if we're not home in the morning, you will need to care for the little ones. I will come back as soon as I can."

Dilnoza nodded. Zumrat patted her head and left the room. She knew Dilnoza would take her responsibility seriously. The oldest children were used to helping care for the little ones.

———

"He must be admitted at once," the doctor on night duty said. "He is a sick boy. How long has he been ill?"

"On and off for the last month. But tonight he got very feverish and I couldn't rouse him," Zumrat said.

"You should have brought him in sooner," the doctor said, his eyes darkening. He followed a nurse as she carried David away from them.

Zumrat wanted to stay with her son, but her request was denied. "He won't know you are there anyway," the head nurse told her. "We sedated him so he will not toss about and rip out his IV. You may as well go home. We will keep watch over him."

By the time they arrived at their apartment building, Zumrat was crying. Abdullah put his arm around her and they climbed the stairs to their third-floor apartment.

Inside all was quiet and dark. Abdullah looked at the clock.

It was almost four o'clock in the morning. He followed Zumrat into their bedroom where they checked on the baby. Her breathing was still labored, and her tiny chest moved up and down rapidly. Johann, too, was tossing restlessly and moaned slightly in his sleep.

Zumrat sank on the bed and covered her face as she wept. Abdullah sat beside her and began praying silently. He let the first storm of tears pass before he said gently, "It's all right to cry, Zumrat. God has told us He hears the cries of the brokenhearted."

Zumrat nodded, but the tears still scorched her eyes, and she reached for a handkerchief. Mopping her tears, she said, "They're not so much tears of questioning, but more tears of being tired. I should be thankful for what we have instead of feeling sad. I do trust in God, and I know He loves us." Just saying it made her feel better.

"I know you are tired of the uncertainty of our life here in Moldova," Abdullah acknowledged thoughtfully. "Now, with the children sick and David on his deathbed, I think you are worn out. It's probably a bigger strain on you than I realize. I want to rest in God's care for us, and yet, even for me, there is always the question of where we will live next. We waited for so long on an answer from the Moldovan government, and when they denied our request, it hit me hard. I so want to provide a home for you and the children."

Zumrat heard the heartache in her husband's voice. Now it was her turn to try to encourage him. "You're doing all you can, Abdullah. God has not forsaken us! I think this is a trial to prepare us for even greater trials. Remember, Jesus said whom God loves, He chastens. Are we willing to be chastened?"

Nodding, Abdullah said, "Yes, even if it means giving up David. I feel like Abraham when he was asked to give up Isaac. That was his only son, but I don't think it would have been any easier if he had had many sons, as we do. I want to be willing to give up any of our children God wants to take."

"At first I did not think I could give David to Him," Zumrat said. "But on the way to the hospital, I found peace and rest and told God in my spirit that I was willing to give up our son if He wanted him in heaven." Once more, tears streamed down her cheeks, but they were not bitter tears.

Abdullah and Zumrat did not sleep the rest of the night, but spent the time praying and committing their family and their future into the hands of God. Even though they felt they were hanging on to their faith by their fingertips, they still trusted in the God who had never forsaken them. In this they found contentment.

"He is totally recovered! It is simply amazing!" The nurse greeted the anxious couple the next morning. "Come, see!"

They eagerly followed her into David's room. In spite of their faith, they were amazed to see their three-year-old son sitting up in bed, playing with a stuffed toy the nurse had given him.

"Mama!" he shouted, stretching out his arms toward her.

"Oh, my David! God gave you back to us! He heard our prayers!" Zumrat wrapped her hungry arms around her son.

"It is surely a miracle. Someone must have heard your prayers," the nurse agreed. "As soon as the doctor has signed the release forms, you may take him home."

"God is so good! God is so good!" Zumrat could not help repeating over and over again. She did not have enough words to express her thankful heart, but she knew she was perfectly understood by the One she addressed.

Chapter 19

With a start, Abdullah sat up in bed. Something had awakened him. He listened, straining to hear. Zumrat was beside him, breathing evenly. Whatever had awakened him must not have penetrated her sleep.

Easing out of bed, Abdullah went to the second-story window and looked out. He could not see anything unusual. He checked his watch. It was midnight. What had awakened him?

He went to the other window, overlooking their yard. All was black outside. No light came from any of the streetlights. *The electricity must be off again,* he thought.

Too wide-awake to crawl back into bed, Abdullah crept down the stairs. He did not want to wake his brother and sister-in-law, so he slipped through the kitchen and out the back door. He did not need any light to traverse the familiar path through his own home.

The warm summer night was silent as he stepped outside. He stretched his arms over his head, but something told him to be quiet, not to make a noise.

This was the second night after their return home to Osh. They had left the children with people from the fellowship in Moldova, and he and Zumrat had traveled back to Kyrgyzstan to "test the waters" to see if the Muslim zealots had quieted down and if it might be safe to move back to their old home.

His youngest brother, Abdumalik, and his wife Nazira had been surprised to see them when they had pushed open their front door and walked in. "What brings you back here?" Abdumalik had asked as Nazira had appeared from their kitchen to see who had arrived.

"Don't let anyone know we are here," Abdullah had told them. "We came back to renew our passports and to see if perhaps we could move back."

At first, Abdumalik and Nazira had told them things were quiet and that they had not heard of any trouble for months. However, Abdullah and Zumrat knew they might not know what had been happening among the believers, for they were not Christians.

"Not good," had been the response the next day when Abdullah had hunted up some of the few believers who remained. "They are still watching us, and we are continually harassed and asked to pay fines."

Then, the next evening, Nazira had begun dropping hints that she had heard the Christians were still in trouble. She mentioned some "troubles" she had heard about that day at work.

"I get the feeling Nazira is hoping we won't stay," Zumrat had said that evening as they prepared for bed. "I think she likes our house."

"We must not think ill of her," Abdullah had replied, trying to quiet his own suspicions.

Now, out in the dark yard, he began to pray silently. "Lord, you know all the difficult situations we have been in. Once more, I want to know from you what we should do. Should we move our family back here to our house? I don't want to be fearful, for in your Word you say, 'Perfect love casts out all fear.' I want to trust in you, yet I do not want to put my family in danger. We need your direction."

Sleep was far from his mind as he prayed.

He prayed that his children would not be negatively affected by all the experiences they had been through. He knew that moving from place to place, making new friends, then moving again was never easy for children. The oldest ones had been attending school in Moldova for two years now. They seemed to be adjusting well, although in the beginning it had been hard. As children often do, the Moldovan students had made fun of the newcomers and mocked them for being different. Then, gradually, the pressure had faded as the foreigners began to blend in.

The fellowship continued to be an inspiration for Abdullah and Zumrat. They felt at home with the believers, and Abdullah was once more used in the ministry. He had joined the local effort to spread the Gospel and preached many messages in the church.

Lost in thought and prayer, Abdullah barely noticed as a bright light shone on the front of their house, his subconscious mind dismissing it as the headlights of a passing car. Then, roused from his meditations as the beam of light slowly traveled from window to window, he stood up and slipped in the back door. The fence blocked his view of the street from the first floor, so Abdullah stole softly up the stairs and into the room overlooking the street. Through the open window, he could hear the sound of an idling car motor. He also heard men's voices. Standing to one side so no one could spot him, he tried to listen.

"... let those reprobates know we are after them."

A chill swept over Abdullah. He could make out four dark forms as they lurched up the sidewalk and tried to open the locked gate. The high-beam flashlight bounced around crazily as the men cursed and tried to force the gate open.

"What is it?" Zumrat spoke quietly from the doorway.

"They are out there. They must have gotten word that we are back." Abdullah hated to even voice his thoughts, but he was certain the men were after him.

The noisy group walked around to the side alley and tried to find another gate, all the while shouting vile threats.

Were Abdumalik and Nazira awake? All was silent downstairs.

"They are drunk," Zumrat whispered. "Oh, Abdullah, we must pray."

They silently clasped hands and began praying in whispers. Trying to block the shouts of the men outside, the two lifted their cries to God.

They heard clanging as someone beat against the gate with a large object. The harsh sounds rang through the night.

Visions of the two beaten men swept over Zumrat. She remembered how horrified she had been to see the swollen and puffed faces that night. "Save us, O Lord! Protect Abdullah!"

When he had been in Sweden, and especially after he had returned, Abdullah had been sure the Muslim extremists wanted to catch him. Because of his active role in the church, he knew he was a wanted man. Now, even six years after they had left their country, he was still being searched out. How had word spread that he was back in Osh? Who could have seen him?

Fear gripped him, and he tried not to believe the answer that came to him. Someone who did not want them there. Someone who would be happy if they never returned. An inside informer.

"O God, help us!" he prayed. "Keep me from having suspicious attitudes toward Nazira. If she is not guilty, lay it not to her charge." Yet, in spite of his efforts, he had a sinking feeling that his sister-in-law had somehow let the radicals know he was back.

The beating against the fence stopped, but the men still shouted and cursed. The light still shone erratically into the upstairs rooms, but the intensity of the men's efforts lessened. Then the car motor roared, and with loud shouts the men drove off.

Abdullah and Zumrat did not sleep the rest of the night. Through the dark hours before dawn, they wept and cried out to God.

"We can't move back here," Abdullah told his wife as he held her close. "I was praying and asking God for direction just tonight, and I have been given the answer—though not in the way I would have chosen. It would be too dangerous for our family to move back here."

Zumrat agreed. "We would not be safe here. We must try to find a place to live somewhere else." Then she was silent as the unknown future stretched out before her, dark and fearful. Where could they go?

"Are you still hoping for a different answer from the Moldovan officials?" she whispered.

Abdullah sighed. "For a long time I have tried to hold onto a glimmer of hope, but I do not think we will be able to live there permanently. After they told us we could stay if we moved from address to address, I knew that was not the way out. How can we move our family all the time? They suggested we could leave Moldova every three months and re-enter, but even they sounded skeptical about whether we would be allowed back in with our children if the border officials checked our passports and saw we had only left their country days ago."

"At least we have our proper Kyrgyz passports," Zumrat reflected.

When they had re-entered their country, they had received an unexpected blessing—new passports.

"These passports are no longer valid," the official had told them after glancing at their old ones. "We are no longer under the Soviet Union." Without further questioning, he had issued them new Kyrgyz passports immediately.

"Just for us," Abdullah reminded her. "The children still have their old ones, and the youngest ones don't even have that. Just their birth certificates."

The future seemed bleak. Their hearts were sore from the scare in the night, and everything seemed to crowd in on them in the dark hours before morning.

"Yet we will trust in God," Abdullah spoke into the darkness. "In all our troubles, we know God does not forsake us. I would still rather have this life with God than the life I left behind. The securities I had then were false, and even though we could live in peace in our country during that time, I did not have peace in my heart. I choose you, God, once more."

They encouraged each other as they prayed together until the morning light began to brighten the eastern sky.

Along with the dawn came the realization that they must once again leave their own country, and the sooner the better. That day, with heavy hearts, they began the 2,200-mile journey west to Moldova, back to their family, and to living one day at a time.

"Here is a letter for you." The visiting evangelist held out a white envelope.

Zumrat took the letter, looking curiously at the handwriting. Then, with a pleased smile, she said, "It's from Maria!"

"Yes," Nicolai said with a grin. "When I told our congregation at home about your family's situation, Maria came to me afterward and began asking questions. 'I know them!' she exclaimed. When she found out I was returning, she asked if she could send a letter along. So here it is."

Zumrat could hardly wait until they got home from church to read the letter. As soon as she got a chance, she opened it and began to read.

To my dear friend Zumrat,

Blessings in the name of Jesus Christ, our risen Lord. I greet you in that name of Jesus, whom we both have learned to trust.

My dear friend, how are you? Brother Nicolai has told me about your family's difficulties, and we are praying daily for you. Oh, Zumrat! How I would love to see you and talk with you and pray with you once more! Many times in the past years I have yearned to see you and learn what has happened with you. I praise God that now I know where you are.

Alexander and I and the children are living here in Germany, and we have a good life. Alexander is busy as a mason, and our children are going to school here. We have a nice house to live in, even if it is not as big as the house we left behind in Osh. Oh, Zumrat, God has been so good to us! There is a Russian church here, and we have godly pastors, as you know since you have met Nicolai.

I will eagerly await a reply from you. We have a telephone, so if you can, please call us. I will enclose the number.

Alexander says you should come to Germany and apply for refugee status here. Perhaps you could make this your home. Wouldn't that be wonderful! But we know God's ways are not our ways, and we rest assured that He will direct you just where He wants you.

We send our love and prayers. Your children must be so big by now! Arnold is now thirteen, so your Daniel must be fourteen. And the girls are surely a big help to you. Oh, Zumrat, how I long to see you!

May God bless you richly,

Maria

Wiping her eyes, Zumrat gave the letter to Abdullah and watched his eyes travel back and forth over the lines as he read. After he finished, she took the paper and read it again.

Looking at her husband, Zumrat tried to stay quiet and wait, but finally she asked, "What do you think? Should we try to go to Germany and ask for refugee status there?"

"We have applied to the United Nations Commission for Refugees, and are still waiting on an answer. I still think it's best if we try to go to the United States. A church there is willing to sponsor us." Abdullah tried to piece together his thoughts.

"But we have tried to contact the United States embassies in two or three countries," Zumrat pointed out. "We have been turned away and given vague answers every time. We have gone from office to office. Where did that get us? Nowhere."

Nodding his head slowly, Abdullah replied. "I know. I have very little faith anymore in government officials. We are just statistics to them, not people. I realize they have many applicants and have to sort through all of them, but that does not help our situation."

Abdullah made a decision. "We will see if we can get visas to visit Germany. If we can find someone to stay with the children, you and I and Daniel will go. I don't know if we will make any progress or not, but it's time to try something new."

The believers in Germany sent formal invitations. Armed with their documents and the letter, Abdullah went to the German embassy to apply for visas.

"But you are not citizens of Moldova. You will have to apply in Kyrgyzstan," the German officer told them.

More drawbacks. More problems. Yet, somehow, God opened the doors for Abdullah, Zumrat, and Daniel to travel to Kyrgyzstan. There they were granted visas, and finally they were on their way to Germany.

"I will gladly stay with the children. Go, and perhaps God will make a home for you in Germany," Tanya had urged them. "We will be fine, won't we, children?"

The seven children had nodded. They loved Tanya. She was a single sister from the church, and she stayed with them whenever their parents were gone. Though it was difficult for them to see their parents leave with their oldest brother, they were excited. Would they finally find a real home in Germany?

Chapter 20

"How did you get into Belgium?" the Belgian agent asked Zumrat through a Russian interpreter.

"Friends brought us in." Zumrat answered with as few words as possible.

The middle-aged agent looked at her intently. "We need all the information we can get. You are applying for refugee status here in Belgium. How did you and your son and husband get into Belgium? You have a Soviet birth certificate. You don't have a passport or any other document to show us."

What should she tell this man? Oh, why had they taken her away from Abdullah and questioned her separately? "We won't tell them we came here from Germany," Abdullah had told her before they came to the office to apply for refugee status. "We will leave our passports with Ronald. When he leaves the office, we will not know where he goes, so we can say we don't know where they are."

She had wanted to say, "That's not honest," but she sensed the pressure Abdullah was under, so she remained quiet.

"How did you get into Belgium?" The question came to her again.

Zumrat did not answer. She felt torn in two. She felt this man wanted to help them, but she did not want to give answers directly against her husband's wishes.

"Please wait outside in the lobby," the agent said after a long silence.

Zumrat tried to remain calm, but inside she was extremely jittery. One part of her hoped that finally they could find a country that would take them in as refugees, while another told her that this time would be no different from any other time they had asked for governmental help.

Abdullah was not in the lobby when she was ushered out, so Zumrat sat on a couch and tried to collect her thoughts.

It had been wonderful to reunite with her dear friend Maria. She and Alexander had welcomed them warmly. When they had gone to church in Germany, they had been surprised by the large number of Russians living there.

In a whirlwind of speaking tours, Abdullah had told their story over and over again. A reporter had interviewed them and written an article about their plight in a magazine that touted human rights.

"Belgium is taking refugees more readily than Germany," Ronald, a man who had taken great interest in their story, had told them. "I will take you to Belgium and you can apply for refugee status there."

Now they were here.

Zumrat hunted for a tissue in her purse. What was keeping Abdullah? What was he telling his officer?

Finally a Belgian officer escorted Abdullah back into the lobby.

"Your request has been denied," the officer told the couple.

"But why?" Abdullah asked through the interpreter.

"I am not at liberty to disclose the reason. I do not make the decision."

Zumrat felt the familiar despair clutch her insides. Turned away once more.

"But, sir," Abdullah pleaded, "if you deport us, we have no place to go. Where will you send us?"

The officer looked at them keenly. "You can go to the refugee camp. Many apply for refugee status more than once." He spoke carefully, measuring his words.

Zumrat instantly understood. "Abdullah. I think he is hinting that we try again later."

Thanking the officer, the two left the office.

The three watched as Ronald left in his car. Then Abdullah, Zumrat, and Daniel climbed the stairs to their assigned room.

The refugee camp in Brussels was not all that bad, Zumrat thought, although their room had been very dirty when they had arrived. She had spent most of the night cleaning, and not until morning had she felt comfortable enough to lie down and get some sleep. They shared a small kitchen with two other families, and once they worked out a schedule, they got along quite well. The one family was from Ukraine, waiting for their application to be processed. The other family was from Iran, and even though they could not communicate with words, they communicated with hand signs and body language.

They had to wait three weeks before they could apply for another hearing. Ronald had left them and returned to Germany.

"I didn't know what to say when they asked how we entered Belgium," Zumrat told Abdullah. "What did you say?"

"I told them I didn't know," Abdullah said. "I really didn't know the road names or the towns we went through in Germany and Belgium to get here, so I felt I could just say, 'I don't know. Friends brought us here.'"

Zumrat was quiet. Then she asked, "What did you tell them when they asked who brought us?"

"I told them Ronald brought us. When they asked for his last name, I said I didn't know how to pronounce it properly in my language. They dismissed me soon after that."

"And when they asked where your passport was?" Zumrat had to ask.

"I told them I didn't know where it was. After all, I didn't know where Ronald was, so I couldn't know where my passport was."

When there was no reply from Zumrat, Abdullah thought the matter closed.

"Was that really honest?"

The question came from Daniel. He did not speak disrespectfully, but asked sincerely.

Abdullah looked at his son, who was almost eighteen. He sometimes forgot how mature his oldest son was. Now the direct question struck deeply into his heart.

Abdullah bowed his head. Finally he spoke. "No," he said slowly, "I see that it wasn't. I was trying by my fleshly efforts to keep things vague, thinking that somehow we would not need to tell them everything."

The three sat in the small room in silence.

"I knew you had reservations about my plan when I first told you," Abdullah said, looking at his wife. "I sensed you were not happy with my decision, but at the time, I felt I could not let the officers know we came from Germany. I was sure they would ask why we did not apply for refugee status in Germany, and then they would want to know how we got into Germany in the first place. I thought that information would hinder our case here, and that they might send us back to await official rejection in Germany. Now I see I was wrong in giving answers that left a wrong impression. I should not have done that. Nothing helped anyway." His shoulders sagged under the weight of their problem. "We'll have to go back to Moldova. From there, I don't know what else to do."

"We can try again in three weeks," Zumrat tried to encourage him. "Perhaps they will listen to us if we tell them exactly what happened. I mean, all the way back to when we first left Osh."

"I see no hope," Abdullah said slowly. "All our petitioning, all our cries for help always come back with a negative answer. How can we keep on asking?" His discouragement was evident.

"I want to tell you our entire story," Zumrat began bravely. This time there was a different agent at the Foreign Affairs Office in Brussels. "I want to tell you just how we came to be here."

Once more, the interpreter translated swiftly.

"Where is your husband?" the official asked, glancing through their file.

"He went back to Moldova to be with our other children," Zumrat answered. "Our oldest son, Daniel, is here with me."

The officer nodded, evidently waiting for her to continue.

"We are from Kyrgyzstan originally. Both my husband and I and our five oldest children were born there. When we became believers in Jesus Christ, our lives changed. We told our relatives and acquaintances about what had happened to us, and many listened. Some repented and turned to Jesus also.

"Then in 1992 Muslim radicals led by Rakhmattula began to persecute the Christians. They severely beat and almost killed two of the men from our church. They began to demand large amounts of money from the believers, and we fled to Uzbekistan in fear for our lives."

On and on, Zumrat told their story—how they had tried to reach Sweden, where Christians had assured them they would help them get established. She told him how they were unable to get the necessary visas to get into Sweden and of their subsequent stay in Moscow.

The minutes ticked by as Zumrat related their move to Ukraine, being denied residency there, then moving to Moldova. "That's where we live now, and when our friends in Germany invited us to come and visit them, we had to go back to Kyrgyzstan to get visas. God graciously opened up those doors, so we went to Germany.

"They told us there that Belgium is accepting refugees more readily than Germany, so we decided to come here. We are looking for a country that will accept us." There. She had said all she knew. She would answer any questions and hide nothing.

Relief swept over her. Zumrat had no idea what response the officer would have, but at least it was a great relief for her weary heart to clear herself. So great was the relief that she found herself beginning to cry. She tried to keep back her tears, but couldn't.

Tears need no translation by interpreters. Tears are universal.

"Dear lady," the officer told her quickly, "I believe your story. Don't cry. I will do all I can to help you."

Zumrat gave a shuddering sob and nodded. After a flurry of words the interpreter left the room and returned with a cup of coffee.

"He says to drink this," the interpreter told her. "He wants to look at your folder some more."

Zumrat sipped the coffee gratefully. The hot liquid calmed her.

"Sir, if we have done wrong, all I ask of you is an official document for me and my eighteen-year-old son to return to Moldova to be with my husband and my children."

The officer held up his hand and continued to study the papers. Finally he said, "I think I can help you. I will attach a special note to your file. I know the person who makes the decision. I will plead your case."

Zumrat did not know how to react. Was it possible that they would be accepted? Hope surged through her.

"It will take time. Go back to the refugee camp and wait. We will contact you as soon as we can."

Taking a deep breath, Zumrat said, "Sir, we made friends with Paul and Edith Yoder and they found a place for us to live. Is that all right?"

Nodding, the officer said, "Just let us know where we can contact you."

Again, Abdullah stood before an official in the United Nations office. Why was he here? They had applied repeatedly for refugee status and been constantly rejected. What point could there be in one more attempt? Still, a Christian brother had encouraged him to try again, so he had come to the United Nations Commission for Refugees to once more present their case. Though Moldova was not accepting refugees as permanent citizens, at least they would no longer be living there as illegal aliens, and without refugee status, he had little hope of obtaining passports and visas for the children so they could join Zumrat in Belgium.

"We were rejected by the Belgian government," Abdullah explained to the official. "We have no place to go." His passport, the children's birth certificates from different countries, and the letters they had written to the United States embassies were spread out on the desk in front of him.

The United Nations officer looked at the paperwork. Finally he gathered all the papers and put them into the folder.

"Your request is accepted. We will register you as refugees under the United Nations Act for Refugees." He began writing on a legal pad.

"Sign here," he said, pushing the pad across the desk.

Abdullah scanned the names on the document. "But my wife and oldest son aren't on here."

Wrinkling his forehead, the officer said, "I don't have their passports or birth certificates. I cannot register them as refugees here in Moldova if their documents aren't here. Bring them to my office and I will register them."

"No, you cannot leave now," the same official who had previously interviewed Zumrat told her. "Your petition is being considered, and if you leave we can not process it."

Zumrat counseled with her friends and prayed desperately. She talked to Abdullah on the phone and they prayed together. Though Moldova offered them temporary sanctuary as refugees, the country was not accepting new citizens. Belgium, on the other hand, was accepting citizenship applications from refugees. But the children could not come to Belgium without passports and visas. It was all rather complicated, especially now that their family was in two different countries.

After much prayer and counsel, they finally reached a decision. Zumrat would stay until her paperwork was finished. The prospect of citizenship in Belgium, they decided, was better than a temporary right to stay in Moldova while they sought a permanent home. Surely if she and Daniel were accepted as refugees in Belgium and Abdullah and the rest of the children were accepted as refugees by the United Nations, the Belgian government would recognize the rest of the family. It should only take a couple of weeks. In Belgium they would be close to their Russian friends in Germany, and they had even been welcomed by a Russian church in Belgium.

Time marched on. Processes that Abdullah's family had thought would take weeks stretched out into months.

"We don't know," was the answer Zumrat received whenever

she traveled to Brussels to find out when their paperwork would be done. "We will notify you." "Wait." "Perhaps soon." Always the hope that, just around the corner, they would get their needed documents.

As the weeks turned into months, Daniel enrolled in a welding school, and Zumrat began cleaning houses for people. In spite of the language barrier, they made friends with Paul Yoder's family. Daniel quickly picked up the Dutch language the Belgians used, but Zumrat struggled to communicate.

It helped to stay busy. Many nights Zumrat cried out her frustrations to God and prayed desperately that their family could be reunited. The obstacles appeared enormous.

Perhaps, if they all were granted refugee status, they could apply to the United States embassy and be granted asylum in the States.

Round and round, night after night, her thoughts spun in dizzying circles. Then, reminding herself that there was not a thing she could do about it, Zumrat would turn to God in prayer and finally gain peace by putting her trust in the Lord. He had never failed her yet. She had no other place to go.

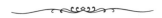

"I missed you all so much!" Zumrat gathered as many of her children in her arms as she could. "I never dreamed it would be more than a year before I would see you all again!" Wiping tears from her eyes, she hugged her youngest daughter tightly. Four-year-old Zoumrad nestled against her mother's side.

"Girls, you have done an excellent job with housekeeping," Zumrat complimented, looking around the orderly apartment with satisfaction.

Dilnoza and Dildora smiled shyly. "But we never stopped missing you," Dilnoza said.

"It was very hard to know how to keep the children happy

sometimes," Dildora said soberly. "I hope we never have to be separated again."

Her heart too full to answer, Zumrat agreed. She and Abdullah had reluctantly decided that she would return to Moldova for a visit and leave Daniel in Belgium. They had little money, but the children needed their mother, so they had agreed that Zumrat should visit. Daniel had stayed behind, both to save money and to be present in the unlikely event that there was a breakthrough in their case.

Abdullah looked at Zumrat and said, "Now we can take your passport to the United Nations office and get you registered as a refugee also."

"But that doesn't mean we can stay in Moldova, does it?" Zumrat asked.

Shaking his head, Abdullah agreed. "It just means we are given recognition as refugees rather than illegal aliens. Perhaps soon we can request immigration at the United States embassy."

Zumrat had barely readjusted to life in Moldova when the call came.

"Mom, that man who was helping you called and said we have to come to his office. Our petition is accepted." Daniel's voice came clearly over the line.

"What?" Zumrat could hardly believe it. *After all this time?*

"Yes," Daniel said eagerly. "Come back to Belgium, and we will be granted residency."

"But," Zumrat said in shock, "I have already been accepted as a refugee here in Moldova. I had thought maybe we could all wait here together as a family . . ."

There was silence on the other end of the line. Then Daniel said, "I don't think they will accept us if you are not here."

"Abdullah, what shall we do?" Zumrat asked.

"The children still don't have visas," Abdullah answered. "Go back to Belgium, complete the registration, and find out if they will let you come live with us until our paperwork is done."

<hr />

"If you go back to live with your family in Moldova, it will be difficult for you to come back here to Belgium," the officer was blunt. "It will be easier for you to apply to get your family to come to Belgium."

Zumrat nodded. Her eyes rested on the papers in front of her. There it was. She and Daniel were now granted the right to live in Belgium.

Then another development made it even more crucial to try to reunite in Belgium. After the terrorist attack on the United States on September 11, 2001, the U.S. froze all applications for asylum in the United States. Their hopes of immigrating to the States were dashed, along with thousands of others'.

Zumrat took Abdullah's and the seven children's official documents to the now familiar office in Brussels. Again she was told that it would take time to process the requests.

Once more, waiting was excruciatingly difficult. The family was again separated, with Zumrat and Daniel in Belgium and Abdullah and the rest of the children in Moldova, all waiting for a country to take them in, waiting for a place to call home.

Chapter 21

"Papa! What's wrong?" Dilnoza bent over Abdullah's bed in concern.

Abdullah opened his eyes and looked at his oldest daughter. "Why do you ask?"

"You were groaning in your sleep." Dilnoza's dark eyes were luminous pools of kindness.

"Oh, Dilnoza. I'm sorry to worry you. I want to be strong in my faith, but I have been going through a difficult time, as I'm sure you realize."

His daughter nodded. He saw tears sparkle in the corners of her eyes.

"I'm sorry," Abdullah repeated. "I know it is difficult for you and Dildora. Between the two of you, you have done an excellent job with the house and the children. I thank you so much."

Dilnoza nodded again and began crying softly.

"We all thought that soon after Mama went back to Belgium, we would get our visas and join her. For almost two years now we have waited, and still we have no definite answer," Abdullah said almost to himself. "If I would have known how this was going to drag on and on, we would never have left Daniel and Mama in

Belgium the first time. But we thought soon we could all live together there."

"Papa, don't fret," Dilnoza said, drying her tears. "You are sick, and getting all upset will not help you. We're all praying for you."

"Thank you. I don't know what we would have done without you. God has been good to us in giving us such wonderful children."

"And we have wonderful parents," Dilnoza said simply. "Even with Mama and Daniel gone, I know we are privileged. Some families that are together have many more problems than we have."

Abdullah closed his eyes. He felt so tired.

"I'll fix you some hot tea," Dilnoza said. "You can drink it whenever you want something." Softly she left her dad's room.

Like an ever dizzying whirlwind, the events of the last two years went around and around in Abdullah's mind.

It had all seemed so simple at first. Zumrat was going to present his and the children's documents to the officials in Brussels. They would see that they had been accepted by the United Nations as refugees. Since Belgium was one of the countries that was accepting refugees, they would be reunited in a short time.

He should have known better, he reflected. When had anything connected to the government ever been quick and simple? After Zumrat had submitted the documents, the officials had seemed to disappear with the papers. "Perhaps soon. We will call you when your case comes up." Again and again, the same discouraging answers.

Why had it seemed during Zumrat's last visit to Moldova that God had led them to send her back to Belgium? Did God really want his wife to be away from the family for two years? Why were their prayers not being answered?

Sick and weary, Abdullah wrestled on into the night. He

heard Dilnoza's soft footsteps as she brought in the tea, but he did not revive himself enough even to say thank you. He was wrestling with a bigger problem. Should he just call Zumrat and tell her to come home? Should he tell her they could not bear it any longer? Whenever they talked on the phone, it was as though somehow, in just a few more weeks, or in a month at the longest, the answer would come. So they had always agreed to wait.

"O Lord," Abdullah was not even sure his words were a prayer anymore, "please tell us what to do! Here I am sick, and not even able to work. The church here has helped us as much as they can, and if it were not for the food packages from the mission in Romania, we couldn't even survive. Bless the people from America who share so faithfully with the needy.

"I feel we are a burden to the believers here. They expect us to leave at any time, so they neglect us because so many other people need help. Please, don't forsake us!" Abdullah lay silent, completely worn out.

As his mind began the ever-familiar circle, retracing the journey that had begun over ten years ago when they had left Osh, his thoughts returned to their first trip to Belgium. This time his thoughts stopped their dizzy whirling and held fast to a point.

I don't know. The answer he had given the Belgian officer now came clearly to him.

Had he not known? Was that the truth?

"I already repented of that," Abdullah objected to the voice that spoke to his conscience. "I told Zumrat and Daniel I was sorry."

There was no answer. Abdullah felt a light shining on a place in his heart that he had not been willing to expose. He had been sorry . . . in a way. At least, he had been sorry his plan had not worked . . .

You want me to answer your prayers. You are asking me to reunite your family. Yet you have not been honest. You lied.

The words seared themselves into Abdullah's brain. *You lied.*

He had known the way they had taken to get to Belgium. He should have told the officer everything. "We came from Moldova to Germany by airplane, then a friend brought us to Belgium from Germany." That's what he should have said.

How often he himself had preached on matters just like this. How often he had exhorted the congregation to be honest in all areas of their lives. "God will not bless shady lives and shady answers." He could hear the echoes of his own messages in his mind.

Now, even as Nathan the prophet had told David when he had caused Uriah's death, the words came ringing into Abdullah's mind. *Thou art the man.*

He was guilty. Guilty of lying.

An enormous burden of guilt swept over the sick and weary man. Abdullah wept.

"Forgive me, my God." The words went winging on their way to the waiting ears of the Lord Jesus Christ. "Forgive me for lying."

By dawn, the sweet peace and assurance that God had indeed forgiven him washed over him once more. Though his body was still weak, his heart was at peace. "Whatever you want from me, I am willing. I once more place our situation into your hands."

Zumrat lay in bed. Darkness surrounded her, but there was no sleep for her tired body. She could hear the late night traffic on the highway, crossing the border between Belgium and France.

How she missed her family! She missed speaking Russian. She was so tired of waiting for answers that seemed to be right around the corner, yet always stayed out of reach. She was tired of the daily struggle with the Dutch language. She was tired of having to make decisions for herself and Daniel without her husband's leadership. She was tired of working long hours with elderly people and with Belgian coworkers whose ways were so different from her own.

She let out a long sigh. Tonight was not a night for tears. She had shed those in the first months when loneliness and frustration had swept over her night after night.

"How can you always stay so cheerful?" her friends asked her. Even though they asked in Dutch, she knew what they were saying. Zumrat just smiled at them.

Cheerful? Try to stay cheerful when your husband and seven children are far away in another country. Try to remain cheerful when repeated requests are answered with "Perhaps soon," and "We will let you know when your papers are ready." *Try that!* she wanted to say, but she could not even remember the Dutch words to say it. So she just smiled.

No one saw the liters of tears she shed over their situation. Only a few knew of the deep anguish she endured during this incredibly long period of waiting. Zumrat did not share her grief readily.

But it was there. Every day, whether at work or in church with her friends or at the little apartment she and Daniel shared, the weight was always there. How could she forget that her family was waiting to come to Belgium? How could she stop thinking of little Zoumrad, now five years old? How could she forget her youngest boys, Johann and David, now seven and eight? Marchamat was almost ten, and surely she needed a mother to help guide her. And Zafar was now thirteen, a teenager.

And Dilnoza and Dildora. They were now eighteen and seventeen, young ladies. Whenever she spoke to her children on the telephone, it took all her strength to keep from bursting into tears, especially when the little ones cried for her.

Even now, thinking about it, Zumrat found that her eyes were wet. She was almost surprised, for she had thought she had no more tears to weep. She felt old and dried up.

"God, I need your help. I am so weary. I don't know if my children need a mother more than I, their mother, need them. I come to you once more. Look down in mercy on your helpless child. You know my deepest thoughts and the mess we are in. I am tired of bringing the same petition to you. Yet I have no other place to go. I have tried all I could at the government offices, and still there is no definite answer. I once more put my trust in you, my Lord and my God."

Only those who have experienced the sweet peace that God gives to those who in desperation cry out to Him for help can know the peace that came to the grieving mother and wife as she again yielded herself to God's perfect will.

Chapter 22

"Come, let's pray before we send off this letter," Brother Gerald told the others.

The small group of believers knelt in a circle in Gerald's home. Zumrat and Daniel knelt side by side.

In spite of the language differences, Zumrat had learned to love and appreciate the believers who met weekly to worship. She felt these people were sincerely serving the Lord. Not only did they tell her they cared for them in their separated situation, they did whatever they could to help.

That was why Gerald had written the letter that was now sealed and ready to be sent—a letter of entreaty to Queen Paola of Belgium.

"She will have pity," Lydia, Gerald's wife, told Zumrat. "The Belgian people know they have a queen who will listen when she gets a petition."

As they all knelt and prayed, Zumrat did not understand all the words the others used in their prayers, but she prayed as she always did, in her own language. Long before, she had learned that God was a loving, caring God—a God who listened to the language of the heart much more than He listened to the language of the mouth. So, in her own way, she poured out her petition that God would soften the Queen's heart and that she would assist them in getting their family back together again.

She knew Abdullah was also praying, as was the church in Moldova. Other people around the world who had been following their homeless journey were praying, and the Christians in America who had been willing to sponsor them had not stopped praying for them.

Zumrat imagined all the prayers of the believers ascending to God, all praying the same thing. "Unite Abdullah's family. Lord, if it be your will, unite this family."

The letter was sent, and even though Zumrat had prayed earnestly, she tried to tell herself not to be too disappointed if this petition did not bring any results either.

"I am willing, Lord, to go back to Moldova, if this is your will," she prayed again. "I want to be in the center of your will."

October 16, 2003

In response to your letter to Queen Paola of Belgium on September 30, 2003, her majesty has directed to favorably address the need of Mrs. Jousoupjanova.

Direction has been sent on October 8, 2003, to the Belgian Embassy in Bucharest, to grant entry visas for the husband and children of this separated family.

Sincerely,

For the Minister of the Director-General,

F. Roosemont

Gerald peered over his glasses at Zumrat. "Do you understand the letter?"

Not quite daring to believe what her friend had read, she looked at Daniel for confirmation. "Yes, Mama," he said in Russian. "You understood correctly."

The Queen had heard their petition. As there was no Belgian

embassy in Moldova, she had given direction to the embassy in Romania to issue visas for Abdullah and the children.

Zumrat was almost bursting with the news. "Hello! Hello!" she almost shouted into the phone. "Dilnoza, is your father there? Tell him to come quickly to the phone." She waited impatiently until she heard her husband pick up the receiver.

"Abdullah! Do you remember that letter we sent to the Queen? She sent a reply! The Belgian embassy in Romania has been directed to issue visas for you and the children! Oh, Abdullah! God is answering our prayers!"

When Abdullah heard the good news, hope once more surged in his heart. Were they finally getting some help? A voice of caution tried to dampen his spirits, yet he could not help but feel a stronger faith than ever before. God was answering their prayers! The Queen herself was interested in helping them!

"We have been working on it," the official from the United Nations assured Abdullah. "Yes, we are clearing visas for your family."

Had they not needed the prompting from the Queen to get the visas moving? Was the official now saying that they would soon have gotten clearance anyway?

Yet Abdullah knew that government agencies didn't like to be caught looking foolish for allowing cases to rest dormant for a long time. He was sure that, whatever he was told, God was using Queen Paola to push the issue to the forefront. So he said nothing, but provided the officer with the names of the children, their birth certificates, and his passport.

"We will put all of your children on your passport," Mr. Antion, the official, told him. "Oh, no. Your oldest daughter is now eighteen. She will have to have a separate passport." He processed the papers as he spoke. "There. Now we are ready to send all the paperwork to Romania, where the Belgian Embassy has to issue the visas." He seemed eager to help.

Abdullah talked with the children, and even though he cautioned them against getting their hopes up too high, they all felt quite excited by the new developments. The Queen—wow! They were quite impressed.

"Mr. Jousoupjanov, I am sorry to inform you, but the documents we received from the Belgian Embassy in Romania do not have all the necessary signatures." Mr. Antion told Abdullah a week later.

A wave of disappointment swept over the listening man. At first he had been thrilled to get the news that he was to come to the United Nations office only a week after he had appeared with the documents. Now this?

"They also question why they are receiving these documents from Moldova instead of from Kyrgyzstan. They sent a letter saying they need to get the documents from Kyrgyzstan since you are not registered in Moldova."

Abdullah's head was spinning. Were they being blocked again? Was this another dead-end street? "What do we do now?" Abdullah tried to keep his bitter disappointment from showing.

A shrug was the only answer he got. It was evident that Mr. Antion did not want to be responsible for what was happening to their family. "That is not my problem."

That night there were many tears as the children heard once more that another barrier had been erected to keep them from going to see Mama and Daniel. Question after question poured out, and Abdullah could only say, "I don't know. We must throw ourselves again on the mercy of God. He changed the hearts of the kings in the Bible, and he can change the hearts of the officials. As hopeless as it seems, we must still keep faith that someday God will reunite us."

"The documents have been sent again to the Belgian Embassy in Romania. We will ask them to waive the fact that they are arriving from Moldova rather than from Kyrgyzstan. We have not abandoned your case." The welcome news came over the telephone as Abdullah called the United Nations office again. Mr. Antion actually sounded interested in helping them.

Abdullah wondered what all was happening behind the scenes. Clearly, the Lord was moving someone to keep their situation from disappearing beneath a pile of papers on an official's desk. "Thank you, Lord," was all he was able to say.

A week later the welcome news came winging its way to their home. Visas would be issued for their family to fly to Belgium to be reunited with Zumrat and Daniel!

In the middle of sharing the wonderful news with the other believers in Moldova and with Zumrat and Daniel and their friends in Belgium, a niggling worry kept bothering Abdullah.

Where could they get the money to buy eight airline tickets to Belgium? He did not have nearly that much money.

"God, I give this need to you. You know just what we need." Over and over again, Abdullah had to pray the same prayer as the paperwork was being completed. Even though their case was to be expedited, the wheels of officialdom still turned slowly. October turned to November, and still they waited. Now that something was actually happening, it was even harder to wait. Yet they were sure their goal was coming closer.

Zumrat made plans with her friends so their family would have a place to stay. Paul and Edith Yoder were moving to another house several kilometers away and offered their former house to Abdullah and Zumrat.

A home of their own, large enough for their entire family to all live together. An almost surreal feeling swept over Zumrat as she eagerly awaited new developments.

As Abdullah retraced the now familiar route to the United Nations office, his booted feet swiftly covered the cold sidewalk. December 10, 2003, he had received the call. "Come, your visas are ready." He had heard the words with both joy and trepidation. Visas!

They still had no money for tickets. How were they to get such a large amount? Even selling their little car would not bring in enough cash for eight tickets.

"Sir, here are your papers. All is in order for you to fly to Belgium on December 23." Mr. Antion smiled as he pushed a folder under the metal grid. "You will be reunited with your wife and son. Congratulations."

Abdullah cleared his throat. He felt short of breath. "What about money to buy the tickets?" There. He had voiced his fear.

"Oh." Mr. Antion waved his hand. "Well, we can send a message to the headquarters in Geneva and request assistance for the funds." Then, with another shrug, he said almost in an undertone, "Not that they usually respond to such requests, but we can try."

Thirteen days passed with no assurance that they would have money to buy the tickets.

"We will carry on by faith," Abdullah told the children as they went about disbursing the little furniture and household articles they had. "God can open the doors for us, just as he made a way for the children of Israel to cross the Red Sea." He said it as much for himself as for the children's sake.

On the sixteenth, Abdullah's phone rang. "We have received money from Switzerland to purchase your tickets." The woman's voice sounded calm and unemotional. "Prepare for your flight on the morning of December 23. We will brief you on more details later."

How could she say those precious words in such a businesslike, unemotional tone? Abdullah's feelings overflowed as he shared the wonderful news with his children. As they prayed, their joyful hearts gave language to their deepest feelings. Had the last hurdle finally been cleared?

Some of the believers from their church accompanied the family to the airport in a van. Others came with public transportation to see them off and to offer words of encouragement. The children were leaving behind five years of ties with their friends. For the youngest ones, Moldova was the closest thing to a home they had ever known.

What would life be like in a foreign country? How would they cope with a different culture and a different language? But pushing those thoughts away was quite easy. They would be with Mama again! With Mama and Papa and Daniel and everyone else! Smiling through their tears, they said their farewells.

"These are tourist visas," the ticket agent remarked, examining Abdullah's passport. "They are not visas to stay indefinitely in Belgium. They expire in thirty days. And yet you have no return date." He looked up at Abdullah. Then, with a shrug, he stamped the papers and shoved them back. That would not be his problem. Someone had issued the visas, and even though they were the wrong ones, the blame would not be on his shoulders.

The tickets. Abdullah tried not to worry. He was kept busy with his children and saying goodbye to the brethren. But they still did not have their tickets. Where were they?

As they waited to go through security, the clock on the wall reminded them that their flight would depart in less than an hour. Pushing down his anxiety, Abdullah once more waited patiently on the Lord for help. He sensed there was a higher power orchestrating these last events. God had proved Himself so faithful in the last three months. Every time a door closed, another door opened somehow.

Nevertheless, he kept scanning the departure hall looking for someone who might have the all-important means for their departure.

There! Was that the contact man? Abdullah was not sure. A man of medium-height was carrying a brown envelope and appeared to be looking for someone.

"Sir," Abdullah approached him, "are you . . . Do you have tickets for me and my family?"

Looking up at him, the man asked, "Are you Mr. Jousoupjanov? Do you have seven children?"

Suddenly Abdullah could not speak. Tears sprang to his eyes, and all he did was nod.

"Oh, great!" The man was clearly relieved to have found Abdullah. "I thought I might miss you, and your flight is due to leave in less than an hour. Here, come this way," he beckoned, and Abdullah rounded up his family and quickly followed his host.

A quick goodbye to their friends, and they lined up and went through security. They checked their bags, then arrived at their gate, where they waited for departure. The children stayed close to their father, their eyes large with wonder at all the bustling around them. There, right outside the huge glass windows, was the airplane that was to take them to a strange country called Belgium! Strange and foreign, yet it was also their promised land, for they had been promised a home there. A place to live, all together. Mama and Daniel would be waiting for them when they landed at the airport. Mama! Daniel! It all seemed like a dream. A wonderful, wonderful dream from which they never wanted to wake.

Chapter 23

Zumrat gripped the handle of her purse tightly with both hands as she watched the stream of people coming through the opening in the arrival hall of the airport. She looked at her watch.

Daniel stood silently beside her, waiting also. Behind them in a semi-circle were their friends, waiting with them. At least twelve people had come to welcome Zumrat's family to Belgium.

Wetting her dry lips, Zumrat smoothed her hair. Time crept by. According to the clock, the airplane should be on the ground. Surely thirty minutes was enough time to have all the passengers off the airplane and into the Brussels terminal. They would have to stand in line and wait their turn to go through customs. Yes, that could take time. Zumrat knew from experience.

She also remembered the tense feeling every time she waited for her turn to face the customs official. Many times she had marveled at how easy it seemed for the other travelers. Walking nonchalantly right up to the officer, they would slide their passports onto the counter, waiting with perfect assurance that there would be no problem. Zumrat always felt her own palms damp from perspiration. Like now.

Lydia smiled at her sympathetically. Zumrat smiled back and felt a little of her nervousness fade. She glanced at the faces of the others.

How good it was to have strong Christian friends here in this new land! Over and over, Zumrat had thanked God for the many new believers she had met. Some she had met only briefly, and with others she had become close friends. They had prayed with her. They had anguished with her every time another door had closed in her face.

With a gentle sigh, she turned again to scan the sea of faces streaming into the arrival hall. "I am as excited as a child!" she chided herself. "I have waited for almost three and a half years for this moment. Surely I can wait a few more minutes!"

Yet every nerve in her body felt on edge, willing her husband and children to come. It was as though all the frustrations, all the waiting times, all the hopes that had been dashed were now rising like a flood, making it almost impossible for her to wait a minute longer. Her heart yearned to see them, to take them into her arms and feel each one of them.

What if, at the last moment, they had been delayed? During their last phone call Abdullah had seemed a little troubled. What if they had never been able to board? Surely they would have called. They had the cell phone numbers of some of her friends. She pushed those thoughts away. They were just in line somewhere, waiting their turn.

Once more, Zumrat turned her thoughts toward how God had never left them or forsaken them through the entire eleven-year ordeal since they had left Osh. Back then she could never have imagined that they would wander from country to country seeking a home.

Yet every time she felt as though she could not face another trial, whenever she cast herself into the care of her Lord and Saviour, Jesus Christ, she knew she was loved. Knowing that, she could place the unknowns, the difficulties, the hardships, and all the other perplexities of life into the keeping of Jesus. Had He not said, "Come unto me, all ye that labor and are heavy laden, and I will give you rest"?

Rest. That was what she was looking for. A place of rest. Now she realized that even though they had been searching for a place to call home, a place where the family could all be together, there was rest even without having that. Her rest was in Jesus, no matter what her circumstances.

"Mama!"

There they were! Coming through the opening! Abdullah! The children!

Then she was on her knees gathering Zoumrad into her arms. She did not try to stop the tears that cascaded down her cheeks as she hugged her youngest child. Without releasing her daughter, she pulled Johann into her arms.

The Jousoupjanov family is joyfully reunited at the airport in Brussels.

223

And David. And Marchamat and Zafar. Oh, her arms were not big enough to gather her precious children near to her heart! She went from one to the other. When Dildora and Dilnoza were in her arms, she realized they were as tall as she was. She hugged them both tightly.

She saw Abdullah embrace Daniel. Then she fell into her husband's arms, while the children all cried and hugged her and Daniel.

This was surely a hallowed spot. Her friends had bravely started singing a song of praise to welcome Abdullah and the children, but before they had even finished the first verse, their voices had died away as their own eyes misted over.

It didn't matter that many a curious eye watched the group in the arrival hall of the airport. All the years and months of pent-up emotions culminated into one glorious reunion. They were together. All of them. In a country that had accepted them. A place they could finally call home.

Pictured (standing, L–R) are Johann, Dilnoza, Zoumrad, Dildora, Zumrat, Canadian pastor, Dmitri Bezpavlov, Daniel, David, and Abdullah, and (kneeling) Marchamat and Zafar, the day of Dilnoza and Dildora's baptism.

That night, after they had eaten and the visitors had all left, Abdullah and Zumrat and their family sank gratefully to their knees. Simultaneously, they prayed. Each of them—father, mother, sons and daughters, from Daniel right down to little Zoumrad—thanked the Lord Jesus Christ for bringing them together. They knew the trials were not over for their transplanted family. They knew there would be hurdles to cross as they blended once more into a family unit. They knew life in a foreign country would not be easy.

However, they knew a much deeper truth that surpassed all the trials they could ever face. God was with them. He had proved to them time and again how much He loved them. In Him they would find the strength and courage to overcome every obstacle this strange new life could bring. In that they rested.

Epilogue

Only a month later, when Abdullah's family went to the city hall to register as they had been instructed to do, they were told, "You only have tourist visas. You do not have permission to live in Belgium." Their papers and passports were confiscated, and in a few days they received a letter that they had one month to leave the country.

The news shocked everyone. They were to be deported? After all the hardships they had gone through to be together?

There was another intense time of praying and fasting. Their friends helped them petition, and finally their documents were returned with an official letter granting them the right to stay in Belgium.

It took seven more months for the slowly turning wheels of bureaucracy to churn out their final residency permits. Finally they were granted the legal right to live in Belgium for as long as they wished.

When the Yoders needed their house again, Abdullah's family faced more difficulties. No landlord wanted to rent a house to a family of ten. Again and again they were turned away.

Then, once more, Gerald wrote a letter to the queen and solicited her help, after which they were respectfully shown a selection of apartments. When they chose a two-story apartment with four bedrooms, they were given an official letter stating that they would be allowed to live there for the rest of their lives if they chose to do so.

The government coffers were opened, and not only did the housing department subsidize the monthly rent on their home, but someone decided that they had been entitled to refugee aid funds all the months since their arrival in Belgium. Since they had not been given this money, they were now given a large sum of money to compensate for the oversight.

Their financial hardships eased for a time, but they had other trials to face.

Not all their neighbors liked having a foreign family with so many children living right in their development. Abdullah's family felt their animosity and tried to be friendly and respectful.

The children were enrolled in school and, as could be expected, had difficulty with the new language and customs of education in Belgium. Even the language courses they took did not fully equip them for integration.

Zumrat continued to work, for Abdullah found learning the language a gigantic burden and could not find work because of it.

Yet all of this did not diminish their joy in being together as a family. They attended a Russian church where they could speak freely and fellowship with other believers. The children made acquaintances and friends once more and learned to cope with the hardships.

They traveled once more to Germany and reunited with Maria and Alexander and their family. With joy, Abdullah and Zumrat watched a friendship develop between their oldest daughter, Dilnoza, and Arnold, the oldest son of their dear friends. In 2006, the young couple married and made their home in Germany.

The saga of the family is not over. The children continue to grow up, and as they mature, they face the same challenges all families face.

What does the future hold for this family that wandered from home to home? How will they respond to the pressures of living in an affluent society, right in the middle of a brand new world?

If they continue to trust in the same God who brought them this far in their journey—the One who has been their Anchor, their Rock, and even their Friend—they will endure until they have reached their eternal home.

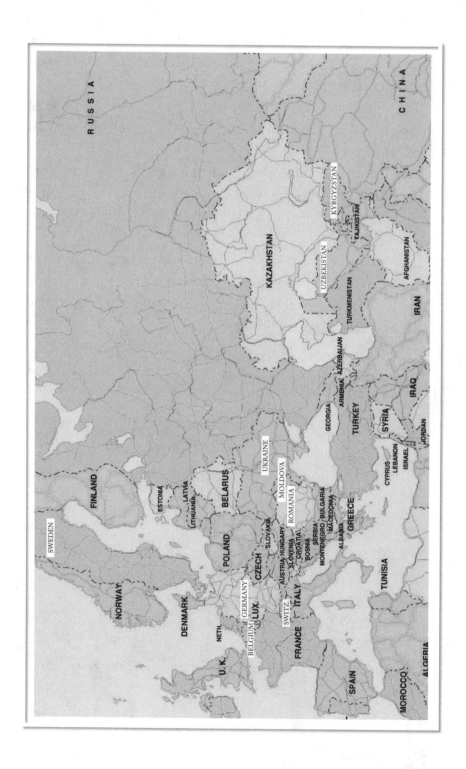

Glossary

Abdulatip	*ahb DOO lah tip*
Abdullah	*ahb DOO lah*
Abdumalik	*ahb DOO mah lik*
Ahmed	*ACH med*
Akbura	*ahk BOO rah*
Allah Akbar	*AH lah AHK bahr*
Anastasiya	*AH nah stah ZEE ah*
Antion	*ahn TONE*
Anya	*AHN yah*
Ari	*AH ree*
Arvat	*AHR vaht*
Aziz	*ah ZEEZ*
Babushka	*BAH boosh kah*
Begzod	*BEG zod*
Bezpavlov	*BEZ pohv luhv*
Chisinau	*kish IN yohf*
Dildora	*dil DOR ah*
Dilnoza	*dil NOH zah*
Dmitri	*DMEE tree*
Elena	*eh LEHN ah*
Elia	*ee lee YAH*
Galina	*gah LEE nah*
Gerald	*JEHR ald*
Girod	*GI rod*
Heinrich	*HINE rikh*
Iosef	*YOH seef*
Ivan	*ee VAHN*
Ivanov	*ee vahn OHV*
jihad	*JI hahd*
Johann	*YOH hahn*

Jousoupjanov	*yoo zoop ZHAN ohv*
Kyrgyz	*keer GEEZ*
Kyrgyzstan	*KEER geez stahn*
Luda	*LYOO dah*
Lyuba	*LYOO bah*
Marchamat	*MARH ah maht*
Margreta	*mahr GREH tah*
Mikhail Ches	*mee khah EEL Chehs*
Miryam	*meer YAHM*
Monat	*moh NAHT*
Nadia	*NAH dyah*
Nazira	*NAH zee rah*
Nicolai	*nee coh LIE*
Oleg	*OH leg*
Olga	*OHL gah*
Rakhmattula	*ROK mah TOO lah*
Rano	*RAH noh*
Ranut	*RAH noot*
Sherzat	*SHEHR zaht*
Shevchenkova	*shyehv CHYEHN koh vah*
Sofia	*soh FEE ah*
Sopia	*soh PEE ah*
Tanya	*TAH nyah*
Tashkent	*TASH kent*
Tatyana	*taht YAH nah*
Ulubek	*OO loo bek*
Uzbekistan	*ooz BEK ah stahn*
Venyamin	*vehn yah MEEN*
Viktor	*VEEK tohr*
Yeveka	*yah VAY kah*
Zafar	*ZAH fahr*
Zina	*ZEE nah*
Zinop	*ZI nop*
Zoumrad	*ZOOM raht*
Zumrat	*ZOOM raht*

About the Author

Harvey was pursuing a writing project in Romania when missionary Nathan Bange told him about a family of fugitives searching for a country to take them in. Zumrat and Daniel were in Belgium at the time, and Abdullah and the other seven children were in Moldova.

Nathan mentioned that someday, when the family was reunited and settled, their story would make a wonderful book.

Struck by this family's hardships, Harvey followed their story through the years. When he finally met Abdullah and Zumrat and their family in 2007, he was impressed by their quiet acceptance of what life had dished out to them. Even peacefully settled in Belgium, Harvey still felt their intangible apprehension that they might have to move again. He sensed the couple's heartache from their constant moving, Zumrat's frustration in not having a settled home, Abdullah's feelings of inadequacy in providing a permanent place, and the children's struggles to cope with their bewildering life.

But as the days of interviews progressed, Harvey was

233

impressed again and again with the family's strong faith. There was so much to talk about, yet the common theme was their faith in a known God through an unknown and trying life. Despite their frustrations in finding an earthly home, they were clearly more interested in seeking a home not made with hands. That recurring theme became Harvey's primary motivation in writing this book.

Harvey and his wife Karen live near the Blue Ridge Parkway in the scenic mountains of western North Carolina. They have been married for over thirty years and have five children and four grandchildren. In addition to his writing, Harvey manages a JCPenney catalog store. He has traveled all over the world writing his thirteen other books, most of which have been published by Christian Aid Ministries and are listed in the back of this book.

Harvey enjoys hearing from readers and can be contacted by e-mail at harveyoder@juno.com or written in care of Christian Aid Ministries, P.O. Box 360, Berlin, Ohio, 44610.

About CHRISTIAN AID MINISTRIES

Christian Aid Ministries (CAM) was founded in 1981 as a nonprofit, tax-exempt, 501(c)(3) organization. Our primary purpose is to provide a trustworthy, efficient channel for Amish, Mennonite, and other conservative Anabaptist groups and individuals to minister to physical and spiritual needs around the world.

Annually, CAM distributes fifteen to twenty million pounds of food, clothing, medicines, seeds, Bibles, *Favorite Stories from the Bible*, and other Christian literature. Most of the aid goes to needy children, orphans, and Christian families. The main purposes of giving material aid are to help and encourage God's people and to bring the Gospel to a lost and dying world.

CAM's international headquarters are in Berlin, Ohio. CAM has a 55,000 square feet distribution center in Ephrata, Pennsylvania, where food parcels are packed and other relief shipments are organized. Next to the distribution center is our meat canning facility. CAM is also associated with seven clothing centers—located in Indiana, Iowa, Illinois, Maryland, Pennsylvania, West Virginia, and Ontario, Canada—where clothing, footwear, comforters, and fabric are received, sorted, and prepared for shipment overseas.

CAM has staff, warehouses, and distribution networks in Romania, Moldova, Ukraine, Haiti, Nicaragua, and Liberia. Through our International Crisis program we also help victims of famine, war, and natural disasters throughout the world. In the USA, volunteers organized under our Disaster Response Services program help rebuild in lower income communities devastated by natural disasters such as floods, tornadoes, and hurricanes. We operate an orphanage and dairy farm in Romania, medical clinics in Haiti and Nicaragua, and hold Bible-teaching seminars in Eastern Europe and Nicaragua.

CAM's ultimate goal is to glorify God and enlarge His kingdom. "... whatsoever ye do, do all to the glory of God" (1 Corinthians 10:31).

CAM is controlled by a twelve-member board of directors and operated by a three-member executive committee. The organizational structure includes an audit review committee, executive council, ministerial committee, several support committees, and department managers.

Aside from management personnel and secretarial staff, volunteers do most of the work at CAM's warehouses. Each year, volunteers at our warehouses and on Disaster Response Services projects donate approximately 100,000 hours.

CAM issues an annual, audited financial statement to its entire mailing list (statements are also available upon request). Fund-raising and non-aid administrative expenses are kept as low as possible. Usually these expenses are about one percent of income, which includes cash and donated items in kind.

For more information or to sign up for CAM's monthly newsletter, please write or call:

Christian Aid Ministries
P.O. Box 360 · Berlin, OH 44610
Phone: 330-893-2428 Fax: 330-893-2305

Additional Books

BY CHRISTIAN AID MINISTRIES

God Knows My Size!   *by Harvey Yoder*
Raised in communist Romania, Silvia Tarniceriu struggled to believe in God. But His direct answer to her earnest prayer convinced Silvia that God is real, and that He knows all about her. This book is excellent for family reading time.
251 pages $10.99

They Would Not Be Silent   *by Harvey Yoder*
In this book, each of the stories about Christians under communism is unique, yet one mutual thread runs throughout—They Would Not Be Silent concerning their devotion to the Lord Jesus.
231 pages $10.99

They Would Not Be Moved   *by Harvey Yoder*
A sequel to *They Would Not Be Silent,* this book contains more true stories about Christians who did not lose courage under the cruel hand of communism. It is our prayer that the moving stories will encourage you and help you to be stronger in your faith in the Lord Jesus Christ and more thankful for the freedoms we enjoy in our country.
208 pages $10.99

Elena—Strengthened Through Trials   *by Harvey Yoder*
Born into a poor Christian family in communist Romania, after harsh treatment at a state boarding school and harassment from authorities for helping in secret Bible distribution, Elena finally decides to flee her home country. Will she make it? A true story.
240 pages $10.99

Where Little Ones Cry   *by Harvey Yoder*
This is a story about war in Liberia. In the midst of the terror that war brings are the little children. Their stories, a few of which are captured in this book, are not of typical, carefree children. Some of these true accounts have happy endings, but sad trails lead them there. The purpose of this book is not to entertain, but to help you appreciate our blessed country more and create awareness of the pain and spiritual darkness that abound in much of Africa.
168 pages plus 16-page color photo section $10.99

Wang Ping's Sacrifice   *by Harvey Yoder*
The true stories in this book vividly portray the house church in China and the individuals at its heart. Read how the church—strong, flourishing, and faithful in spite of persecution—is made up of real people with real battles. Witness their heartaches and triumphs, and find your own faith strengthened and refreshed.
 191 pages $10.99

A Small Price to Pay   *by Harvey Yoder*
Living in the Soviet Union under cruel, atheistic communism and growing up during World War II, young Mikhail Khorev saw much suffering and death. Often homeless and near starvation, he struggled to believe in God's love. This inspiring story of how Mikhail grew to be a man of God, willing to suffer prison for the God who loved him, will move you to tears and strengthen your faith. You, too, will come to realize that everything we can give to the Christ who saves us is still . . . A Small Price to Pay.
 247 pages $11.99

Tears of the Rain   *by Ruth Ann Stelfox*
The moving story of a missionary family struggling to help some of the poorest people in the world—the men, women, and children of war-torn Liberia. Vividly descriptive and poignantly honest, this story will have you laughing on one page and crying on the next.
 479 pages $13.99

Tsunami!—from a few that survived   *by Harvey Yoder*
Just like that, one of the greatest natural disasters in modern history approached the city of Banda Aceh, Indonesia. For most people, the cries of "Water!" reached them too late. But some survived to tell the story.
 As you read the accounts in this book, you will experience, in a small degree, a few of the horrors that the people of Banda Aceh faced. Some tell their stories with sorrow and heartbreak, others with joy and hope.
 168 pages $11.99

The Happening   *by Harvey Yoder*
The shootings at the Nickel Mines Amish schoolhouse shocked the nation and the world. This is the heartrending story of the young victims, their families, and the community as they struggled to come to grips with this tragedy. How could they find peace and forgive the man who had caused their grief? The true details of *The Happening* are woven into a story told through the eyes and heart of a young survivor.
 173 pages $11.99

A Greater Call *by Harvey Yoder*

Born into a poor family in famine-racked China, young Wei was left to die. But God had a different plan. Wei would one day answer a greater call. The cost would be enormous, but to Wei and other Chinese Christians, Jesus Christ was worth any sacrifice.

195 pages $11.99

Angels in the Night *by Pablo Yoder*

Pablo's family had endured more than a dozen robberies during their first two years as missionaries in Nicaragua. But God had called them to Waslala, and they had faith that He would protect them.

In spite of the poverty and violence that surrounded them, a fledgling church was emerging, and a light, small at first but growing steadily, was piercing the darkness.

Angels in the Night continues the story begun in *Angels Over Waslala*, chronicling the trials and joys of this missionary family.

356 pages $12.99

HeartBridge *by Johnny Miller*

The Nathaniel Christian Orphanage in Romania opened its doors in 1992 as a home for hurting children. By the time Johnny and Ruth Miller arrived to be tata and mama, the orphanage housed 53 precious children. These are the touching—and sometimes heart-wrenching—stories of the Millers' first year in Romania.

272 pages $12.99

STEPS TO *Salvation*

The Bible says that we all have "sinned and come short of the glory of God" (Romans 3:23). We sin because of our sinful nature inherited by Adam's sin in the garden, and this sinful condition separates us from God.

God provided the way back to Himself by His only Son, Jesus Christ, who became the spotless Lamb that was "slain from the foundation of the world." "For God so loved the world, that he gave his only begotten Son, that whosoever believeth in him should not perish, but have everlasting life" (John 3:16).

To be reconciled to God and experience life rather than death, and heaven rather than hell (Deuteronomy 30:19), we must repent and believe in the Son of God, the Lord Jesus Christ (Romans 6:23; 6:16).

When we sincerely repent of our sins (Acts 2:38; 3:19; 17:30) and accept Jesus Christ as our Saviour, God saves us by His grace and we are "born again." "That if thou shalt confess with thy mouth the Lord Jesus, and shalt believe in thy heart that God hath raised him from the dead, thou shalt be saved" (Romans 10:9). "For by grace are ye saved through faith; and that not of yourselves: it is the gift of God" (Ephesians 2:8).

When we have become born again in Jesus Christ, we must be baptized and then be careful that we do not go back to our sins, since we are new creatures (2 Corinthians 5:17). "He that hath my commandments, and keepeth them, he it is that loveth me: and he that loveth me shall be loved of my Father, and I will love him, and will manifest myself to him" (John 14:21). It is important to fellowship with a faithful group of believers to strengthen and enhance one's Christian walk (1 John 1:7). Enjoy new life in Christ and be faithful and grow in Him (1 John 2:3; Romans 6:13; Revelation 2:10b).